WORKSHOP 3
by and for teachers

THE POLITICS
OF PROCESS

edited by
Nancie Atwell

HEINEMANN
Portsmouth, New Hampshire

Published by
Heinemann Educational Books, Inc.
361 Hanover Street   Portsmouth, NH 03801-3959
Offices and agents throughout the world

Every effort has been made to contact the copyright holders for permission to reprint borrowed material where necessary. We regret any oversights that may have occurred and would be happy to rectify them in future printings of this work.

ISBN 0-435-08576-X
ISSN 1043-1705

Designed by Wladislaw Finne.

Printed in the United States of America
10 9 8 7 6 5 4 3 2 1

CONTENTS

ABOUT
WORKSHOP 3

*W*orkshop 3 is the third in a series of annual volumes that address a current topic in the teaching of reading and writing. The theme of *Workshop 3* is The Politics of Process.

Whenever we talk about education we are talking about politics. Schools are the storehouse of a community's values, beliefs, and biases, and politics enter in determining exactly where those values, beliefs, and biases lie. Often the political discussion takes the form of a debate between two extremes: traditional or nontraditional classroom structures, ethnocentrism or multiculturalism, content or process, phonics or whole language. Teachers who have successfully adopted progressive approaches to teaching writing and reading understand the complex nature of language learning and reject either/or dichotomies. They investigate and acknowledge the values, beliefs, and biases of the communities in which they teach, and work to create opportunities for parents to see their children's school experience with new eyes. The teachers use unambiguous language that describes what they want for children, insist on high standards of excellence in reading and writing, collect and show samples of student work that reveal what occurs in their classrooms, and make the community part of their responsibility as teachers.

This volume describes the efforts of teachers and administrators who have engaged in the politics of process, with varying degrees of success, in order to teach writing and reading as they believe they should. As politicians, the contributors to *Workshop 3* have joined forces with like-minded colleagues, invited dialogue with parents and administrators, negotiated for permission to improve their teaching, displayed their successes, admitted their failings, and even contemplated leaving a school system that required them to teach poorly in order to prepare children for more poor teaching. And they talk straight, as *teachers of reading and writing*, without wrapping themselves in the ambiguity of vogue labels.

Workshop 3 begins with two letters to parents that demonstrate how teachers can use specific language and anecdotes to help the community understand innovative approaches to reading and writing. In "An Invitation to Bake Bread," Linda Hughs acknowledges how difficult it is for parents who were taught one way to have their children taught another. By sharing recollections of her own elementary school experience, she reminds parents that the "good old days" of education weren't all that great. And without resorting to jargon, she paints a vivid, reassuring picture of what parents would see and hear in her fifth-grade classroom.

Mary Ellen Giacobbe's article is a letter to parents of primary grade students about the temporary or invented spellings of young writers. Mary Ellen helps parents focus on what beginning writers can do and explains why they should respond to children's first attempts at writing just as they responded to their early speech. Through examples from her experiences as a teacher and mother Mary Ellen anticipates the concerns that parents might have and helps them to understand what she understands when she reads a child's temporary spellings.

Wilfrid Gordon McDonald Partridge, Hattie and the Fox, Night Noises, Koala Lou, and *Shoes from Grandpa* are valentines to children, parents, and teachers from a writer who loves language and stories. In An Author's Perspective, Mem Fox describes how her writing has been misused in the name of whole language, a term she rejects as misleading and inexplicit. Instead, she offers *real language*—real reading, writing, speaking, and listening— as the goal of teachers who wish to nurture language learning. Her article is a challenge to be wary of slogans and programs as substitutes for thinking about and communicating what we expect of the students in our classrooms.

Teachers at Stratham Memorial School in Stratham, New Hampshire, tackle the subject of evaluation. Portfolio assessment is a hot topic in current discussions of educational reform, but we have few practical models of how a classroom teacher has incorporated portfolios in meaningful ways. Drawing on the portfolio of a parent who is an interior decorator as a real-life model, Mark Milliken and his fifth graders developed an assessment procedure that allowed students to investigate their growth as learners in every subject area and to communicate it to their teacher and their parents. Mark's story shows how a thoughtful teacher, one who trusts students and understands that change takes time, can make his own sense of an educational trend without waiting for an expert to tell him what to do, and how a teacher can invite and respond to parental criticism without compromising his beliefs.

Lynn Parsons makes sense of another educational trend in her article about Stratham's report card. Lynn and a faculty committee redesigned their reporting system to reflect their knowledge of the relationships between reading and writing. Looking beyond "the reading-writing connection," they explored what good readers do, what good writers do, and the parallels that exist between the two. The most recent version of their report card, included here, demonstrates their beliefs about literacy, their expectations of children, and their determination to make their beliefs and expectations the basis of their communication with parents.

Workshop 3 includes a new feature for this series, two guest essays contributed by teachers at the college level. It is my great good fortune that Tom Newkirk occasionally sends me drafts of his writing to read. "The Middle Class and the Problem of Pleasure" began as a speech that Tom sent along last summer, and he agreed to refashion it for inclusion here. In broaching directly the question of why some middle-class parents have trouble with process approaches to reading and writing, he identifies a conflict in the goals they have for their children. While on the one hand middle-class parents are generally permissive, they are also fearful of spoiling their children, and they look to the schools to inculcate self-discipline by making children engage in rote and regimented tasks that will prepare them to meet the entrance requirements of the middle class. Tom argues that it is time for teachers of reading and writing to reclaim the standards argument and, in dialogue with their communities, to emphasize self-discipline through immersion in reading and writing, the teacher's high expectations for young readers and writers, and the joys of work.

Tom Newkirk's theory helped me to account for the popularity of the recent best-seller *Among Schoolchildren* (Kidder 1989) among the middle-class reading public. The classroom depicted in the book practically honors tedium—in the form of endless workbooks, worksheets, and textbooks—as Kidder extols the virtues of a type of teacher that most parents recognize as "good," one who coerces, manages, maintains order, and collects and corrects homework. *Among Schoolchildren* earned most of its rave reviews from people who spend little, if any, time among schoolchildren. But in their reviews, such teachers and researchers as William Ayers, Sara Freedman, Herb Kohl, and Susan Ohanian deplored the joylessness of this classroom and the author's eagerness to blame children's failures on the poverty of their families rather than the poverty of the curriculum. In *Small Victories* (1990), another recent book about a public school in an urban setting, Samuel Freedman depicts a different kind of good teacher. Jessica Siegel taught English on New York's Lower East Side. The skills of her mostly immigrant students were marginal, but there was nothing marginal about her curriculum or her expectations. Siegel's thoughtfulness and passion, the richness of her curriculum, and her invitation to students to think and write and become engaged with literature helped learning make sense and made middle-class success a real possibility for her kids: ninety percent of Seward Park students go on to higher education or military service. The public needs more portraits of teachers like Jessica Siegel to help them redefine good teaching. And chances are that teachers of reading and writing ourselves will have to take the lead in writing about our classrooms in order to show parents that we have not lowered our standards or abandoned their values.

In "Setting the Stage," teacher Mimi DeRose demonstrates how a whole faculty can communicate its priorities to a middle-class community. Although she describes how she and her colleagues gained support for the language arts curriculum of a brand-new elementary school, the public relations campaign they developed has implications for teachers in every setting. Rather than waiting for challenges to their methods, the staff created opportunities for parents to understand and participate in decisions about the school, including methods of evaluation, annual goals, and grant proposals. While their hard work has definitely paid off, it has also led to the realization that public relations is never-ending—and that the ongoing effort actually benefits teachers by causing them continually to reevaluate their methods.

The teacher interview in *Workshop 3* celebrates the efforts of two teachers who have struggled with the same need to earn community support. Two years ago Toby Curry and Debra

Goodman initiated a whole-language magnet school in inner-city Detroit. In this interview by Yetta Goodman, with commentary by Ken Goodman, the teachers discuss the success of their minority students as writers and readers, the objections of minority parents to process approaches to teaching writing and reading, their power as creators of curriculum, and the politics of compromise. It is a tough-minded discussion of issues of responsibility and control and a realistic overview of what it takes to maintain a curriculum that values real language.

In a third account of how a school built support for its teaching of reading and writing, Sig Boloz, principal of a Navajo reservation school in Ganado, Arizona, describes how he and his staff overcame both the geographic isolation of the school and the expectations of parents that their children would be taught as they had been taught. Theirs is a lively, multilayered approach to public relations, in-service training, curriculum development, and evaluation. It is also another challenge to the view that successful writing and reading are restricted to schools in rural New England. Ganado Primary School has been named one of Arizona's ten outstanding elementary schools, an Arizona Exemplary Literacy Site, and a National Lead School by the National Council of Teachers of English.

Patrick Shannon, author of *Broken Promises: Reading Instruction in Twentieth Century America* (1989) and *The Struggle to Continue: Progressive Reading Instruction in the United States* (1990), is the other guest essayist. Pat's article is partly a story of the values, beliefs, and biases of my own community in rural Maine. Two years after I resigned my position as a teacher at Boothbay Elementary School, I asked my former colleagues and the principal if they wished to collaborate with me on a new writing and reading project. Twenty teachers volunteered. I wrote a proposal that spelled out what we would do together at no cost to the school system and asked that it be included on the agenda of the next meeting of the school committee so that we could present our plan for discussion. Shortly after the meeting, I withdrew the proposal.

During my twelve years at Boothbay, the school committee and superintendent had trusted and respected teachers and had allowed us to learn together. The current superintendent and several of the new committee members held no such lofty ideals. One suggested that the teachers who chose to work with me were not smart enough to develop methods and use them effectively. Another was the daughter-in-law of a representative of the

Spalding Foundation, an Arizona-based group that advocates intensive phonics drill. The atmosphere was so poisoned it could never have supported a project like the one I had proposed. No combination of words or examples would change those minds, and I had been naïve to assume that the force of my rhetoric could sway them. Previous to this experience I hadn't felt much sympathy for teachers who complained about oppressive administrators. Now I understood how members of an administration could prevent a faculty from teaching as they believed they should. I was told by a sympathetic school committee member that my proposal would have been accepted had it come to a vote, but by then I understood that the siege mentality of the others destroyed any chance for a successful project.

The story doesn't end there. A year and a half after this episode, a letter to the editor appeared in the *Boothbay Register*, our local paper. It was from Patrick Groff, a retired professor from San Diego State University, who attacked me, my proposal, and whole language and congratulated the school committee on its good judgment. I discovered that Groff, a hero of the Reading Reform Foundation, writes letters about phonics to newspapers at the behest of individuals who believe that an outside "expert" with a Ph.D. will impress the locals. Since I had had no further involvement with the Boothbay schools, I can only guess that someone wanted to intimidate the teachers of reading and writing still working there. I responded to Groff's charges, and, sure enough, a month later another letter from him appeared in the newspaper.

Pat Shannon added Groff's letters to his file documenting the ways in which individuals and groups with a pro-phonics agenda are using various media to influence school boards, voters, and politicians. The lessons that Pat finds in the purposes to which these writers put their literacy are crucial for teachers of reading and writing who wish to gain support for their methods. Groff, Samuel Blumenfeld, Senator William Armstrong, Phyllis Schlafly, and others make their voices heard. They do not speak only to each other, and they avoid jargon that will confuse and alienate the public: in the pro-phonics publications, teachers teach, they do not "facilitate the learning process"; and children learn, they are not "empowered as risk-takers." Pat's article is an invitation to educators to stop blaming the reading reformers for the efficacy of their tactics and to start using literacy as the reformers do, as participants in democracy.

Ed Kenney's article, "Change the Word *Screw* on Page 42," is an account of his perseverance as a participant in democracy. In the context of his principal's creation of an ad hoc committee to censor a collection of student writing, Ed explores the vulnerability of English teachers in rural areas. His response is to use the tools at his disposal (the Washington State Coalition Against Censorship, the ACLU, and his colleagues) to confront those who would deny him and his students their voices, to become even more visible as a teacher of writing and publisher of student writing, and to become more active in his local teachers' association.

In another article about publishing student writing, Marguerite Graham, a writing program director, considers a project gone haywire, a districtwide anthology that grew so big, she and her colleagues lost control of its quality and lost sight of the reasons they had created it. The publishing guidelines that grew out of their experience are modeled on those of professional publications. These guidelines acknowledge that, while kids do need audiences beyond the teacher for their writing, extravagant projects are often no more effective than the single photocopy that will allow a piece of writing to be read by the right person.

In The Author Interview, Ralph Fletcher, a teacher trainer and the author of *Walking Trees* (1991), speaks with Bill Martin, Jr., another writer beloved of children and an advocate for real language teaching. Martin talks eloquently about children's need to hear narratives and poetry read aloud and to be surrounded by adults who tell stories, act, write, and encourage students to do the same in order to create "a language bank for a lifetime." He makes a point similar to Tom Newkirk's: skeptical parents "need to get caught up in the joy of seeing their children develop the necessary skills of the culture," and teachers need to devise opportunities for this to happen.

Workshop 3 closes with a portrait of an exemplary teacher of reading and writing by a high school English teacher who knows her well. Margaret Queenan struggles to define what it is about her cousin, Carol Brennan, a fifth-grade teacher, that turns Carol's students into astonishing writers. Her dinners with Carol reveal a complete professional—a teacher comfortable with her own literacy, a teacher who decides what's important for her and her students to spend time on, a teacher whose active collaboration with students as a reader and writer makes it possible for them to attain her standards. A quote from Plato captures the secret of Carol's effectiveness: "What is honored in a country will be cultivated there." Because she honors good reading and writing, she makes it possible for her students and their families to do the same. Carol Brennan reminds us that the best public relations scheme is no substitute for a teacher who knows what he or she is doing, and why.

One striking thing about this collection is the range of political options available to teachers of real language. Just as there is no one way to teach reading and writing, there is no one course of action to pursue in protecting our methods and a student's right to discover what literacy is good for. As teachers, we must become adept at reading our communities and schools and then ask ourselves some hard questions. How much can we change? In whose company? Where can we compromise, and where will we draw the line? What political strategies are available to us?

Many. Teachers can unite behind good school board candidates and do everything we can to see that they are elected. We can look beyond local politics to legislative, gubernatorial, and presidential campaigns, realizing that the conservative agenda does not bode well for approaches to literacy that challenge children to think, ask questions, and take positions and that we must take our message to the larger arena. We can join our teachers' unions and negotiate for our right as professionals to shape our curricula. We can demonstrate what our students *can* do by keeping sample writing folders, lists of conventions they have learned, lists of the kinds of writing and reading that show up in our classrooms, and lists of the concepts we have introduced in conferences and mini-lessons, and we can ask our critics to compare these data with anybody's scope and sequence of skills. We can invite local authorities, including our colleagues and experts from our universities, to speak in support of our positions, and we can avoid meaningless references ("I'm doing Graves"; "I'm an Atwellian"; "I'm a process teacher") in defining our approaches. If worse comes to worst, as Debi Goodman observed, we can "quit these jobs when they're no longer working for us, when we reach the point where there's too much compromise." We can walk away from school districts that depend on oppressed teachers oppressing students.

Last fall, former Boothbay teachers Susan Stires, Donna Maxim, and I opened The Center for Teaching and Learning, a private elementary school in Edgecomb, Maine. Maine is our home. We wanted to stay here and continue to work with children, but we were not willing to submit ourselves or our students to the whims of a school board that believed its job was to tell us how to do ours. We hope that the hard work of starting a school from scratch will be made worthwhile by our ability to create and disseminate a model that works for teachers and children, one that doesn't depend on commercial materials in any subject area yet still meets state guidelines, one that replaces learning activities with genuine learning. We have attracted a heterogeneous group of kids whose families represent every walk of life, and we will demonstrate, write, and speak about what we do at the school in hopes of showing what is possible across the disciplines. It is a heady undertaking tempered by a sobering sense of responsibility. If we fail, we have no one else to blame. But if we succeed, the fruits of our labors are our own.

"To Be of Use," a poem by Marge Piercy (1973), serves as a kind of epigraph to our work at the school. It ends, "The pitcher cries for water to carry, and a person for work that is real." This volume of *Workshop* represents the experience of teachers of reading and writing who are determined to make their work in classrooms mean something, to make it fulfilling for themselves and memorable for their kids, to make it real.

References

Kidder, Tracy. 1989. *Among Schoolchildren.* Boston: Houghton Mifflin.

Fletcher, Ralph. 1991. *Walking Trees: Teaching Teachers in the New York City Schools.* Portsmouth, NH: Heinemann.

Fox, Mem. 1985. *Wilfrid Gordon McDonald Partridge.* Brooklyn, NY: Kane/Miller.

———. 1986. *Hattie and the Fox.* New York: Bradbury Press.

———. 1988. *Koala Lou.* New York: Harcourt Brace Jovanovich.

———. 1989a. *Night Noises.* New York: Harcourt Brace Jovanovich.

———. 1989b. *Shoes from Grandpa.* New York: Orchard.

Freedman, Samuel G. 1990. *Small Victories.* New York: Harper & Row.

Piercy, Marge. 1973. "To Be of Use." In *To Be of Use.* New York: Doubleday.

Shannon, Patrick. 1989. *Broken Promises: Reading Instruction in Twentieth Century America.* Granby, MA: Bergin and Garvey.

———. 1990. *The Struggle to Continue: Progressive Reading Instruction in the United States.* Portsmouth, NH: Heinemann.

Editor's Note

Because of the responsibilities of a new job I have had to make some difficult choices about my professional life. This will be my last volume of *Workshop.* I loved editing the series and learned much from the contributors to the first three volumes. I am delighted that my friend and collaborator Thomas Newkirk has agreed to serve as editor of the *Workshop* series. Tom is uniquely committed to tapping and furthering the expertise of classroom teachers. I look forward to the insights and perspective that he will bring to the series.

N.A.

*A*nyone who has begun to think
places some portion of the world in jeopardy.
John Dewey

*I*f there is no struggle
there can be no progress.
Frederick Douglass

1

AN INVITATION TO BAKE BREAD

LINDA HAZARD HUGHS
Shelter Rock Elementary School
Manhasset, New York

*D*ear Parents,

We all know that September brings both excitement and dread to children as they wonder what school will be like this year. My son has always had trouble sleeping the night before the first day of school, so I try to be encouraging and supportive. But inside myself I wonder: Will this year hold all that I hope for him?

Last year I was running late on the first day of school, and as my car snaked around the streets of my neighborhood, I met a school bus stopped to pick up a child. A little boy was going off to school for the very first time, I could tell: his dad was giving him that paternal nudge. As the child climbed the steps into the big yellow bus, the father waved and smiled with the confidence that it would be all right. I realized that all over the community that day, parents like me were sending their children off to a new experience with a new teacher, and for many parents and children, I was that teacher. I was the person those parents were trusting to guide and nurture their children.

Our own memories of school are often still vivid in our minds. They can bring a rush of excitement, a feeling of unease, or any one of a multitude of responses to school. And so I wonder when parents walk into my fifth-grade classroom: Are they imagining their children around the tables, on the rug, and in the beanbag chairs, or are they remembering, as I do, their own fifth-grade teachers' classrooms with rows of neatly spaced desks, where we sat in alphabetical order and passed papers back and forth just so? In the same way that I remember the challenges that Mrs.

17

Collins offered me in second grade as a math student and again as an actress when she gave me the lead in our class play, we parents bring our own histories with us when we face our child's teacher. Because we strive for a better life for our children, these classroom memories become important.

My mother says that I was born with a red pencil in my hand: her metaphor for teaching. From the very beginning I subjected my younger brother to playing school, and I was always the teacher. When I went to kindergarten, I came home the first day crushed because I hadn't learned anything new. My childhood was spent learning and practicing the skills I thought I'd need to be a good teacher. And now that I have been teaching for fifteen years, I still ponder my childhood classrooms, wondering what I bring to my classroom from those roots. Clearly, my classroom diverges from the ones that I remember.

In October of first grade, Mrs. Johnson assigned us to reading groups: bluebirds, cardinals, and robins. It took only a few days before we all knew that the kids in the bluebirds were the smart ones. The other two groups were left to figure out where they stood, and soon the robins knew they were the lowest group. So while the bluebirds skimmed along from one basal reader to another, the robins struggled—word by word, page by page—through the first one. Of course, Mrs. Johnson never let the bluebirds talk about how good it felt to be in the top reading group, but she didn't encourage the robins to express their confusion about learning to read either. As parents now, Mrs. Johnson's students send their own children off to first grade. Which reading group would they want their child to be in?

I want you to know that the children arriving in my class will also find reading groups, but the groups will be chosen based on their interests. Last year, in anticipation of a visit from Avi, a writer of appealing books for upper-elementary children, we began to explore his writing and his life as a writer. I chose *Captain Grey* and read it aloud each day, sharing my love for the story and the way it is written. I gathered his other books and gave short book talks about each of them. Each student decided which book he or she preferred to read, and groups emerged. As we continued to read, each group met to talk about the experience of reading their particular book.

In Avi's book *The Fighting Ground*, a compelling story of a boy who confronts the issue of war at the hands of the Hessians during the Revolutionary War, my reluctant readers Brian and David were fascinated that the book was arranged by time rather than by chapters. "I can't stop reading," David admitted. " '9:58, 10:15, 10:25, 10:45'—it's amazing. Time flies!"

"Me, too!" agreed Brian. "Did you get to the part when Jonathan meets his father's friend. . . ."

"Sh-h-h," Shaneeqa whispered. "I'm not there yet."

Later they turned the page and discovered that the Hessian soldiers don't speak English, for suddenly a foreign language appeared in the text. "What *is* this?" Brian demanded.

"It looks like French," Shaneeqa suggested. "But how am I supposed to read it?"

"Well, it sort of makes sense when you read what Jonathan says. Look . . ." and Tory was off, explaining the strategy of reading ahead. Then Brian found the translation in the back of the book, and all four readers attacked the German with a new appreciation.

"Why did Avi use the real German?" I asked, as I joined the group to wrap up the day's reading. I had just come from the group reading *A Place Called Ugly*. They were nearly finished, and we had discussed our predictions about the ending and looked for evidence from the story to support our opinions.

Of course, as children overhear the questions and comments of their peers about different books, new groups form and the process continues. Sometimes the group creates a project to show off their book, prepares an oral interpretation of a scene, or acts out the narrative in dramatic form. But for me the key factor for grouping is children's interests.

Other activities demand different groupings. If my goal is a writing lesson based on Avi's books, groups might form for newspaper, diary, drama, or poetry as we explore styles of writing. I know that learning is based on the child's interaction with the text and his or her experience with it. My knowledge of kids' strengths and weaknesses also determines classroom groupings as I seek to encourage maximum learning. I put kids of varying abilities together, searching for combinations that click. Which child is the patient listener? The insightful thinker? Which reader is the skillful tactician? The groups reflect my awareness that kids learn from kids, that children will learn best when they want to learn, and that all children want to learn how to read and write.

I remember few writing experiences from my first-, second-, and third-grade years. I don't remember writing poetry (or reading it, for that matter). I do remember workbook page after workbook page of skills that I often understood after the first model. I'd finish among the first three, and then all three of us would squirm impatiently like kids waiting for the ice cream maker to stop whirring on a hot summer day. Reviewing those pages later, when everyone was done, was torture as the teacher patiently explained the answers over and over again.

As we moved along in the grades, more attention was paid to composition exercises. Miss Kelly, in grade four, would assign a composition topic and instruct us to write a story. We'd sit silently at our desks and write. When the time was up, we'd hand the papers in to be graded. Days later Miss Kelly would hand the stories back. We'd look at the grade, and she'd admonish us to read her comments. Then she'd conduct a rewriting experience: we would copy our story over again, paying attention to her red revising remarks and corrections. Miss Kelly selected the best stories for the classroom bulletin board. I don't remember my friend John's papers ever being displayed.

In my classroom we write every day. We choose topics that we want to write about and we write. During writer's workshop we practice the craft of writing. We grapple with issues of audience and voice, tense and tone, metaphor and meaning. Since I view each one of my students as a writer, and because I write too, our classroom truly becomes a language laboratory. Each day I provide a focus through a whole group mini-lesson prepared to meet the needs of my writers. One lesson may be about effective leads while another stresses commas in compound sentences, but whatever it is, it has its roots in what I call our "need to know" philosophy: What do these writers need to know to improve the pieces they are working on? Following this ten-minute lesson, we move on to our laboratory time, during which each writer works on his or her writing.

Last year, when Kristen wanted to confer with Cara about her narrative on losing her first tooth, Cara was ready because her draft about winning a gold medal skiing needed an audience. Kristen read her story to Cara, and Cara responded in two ways: she told Kristen what she liked about her piece, and she asked the questions the story left unanswered for her as a listener. Kristen jotted these down to use later, when she revised. Then Cara shared her writing. When both girls had finished, they each worked independently to begin their revisions.

In the same class, Christine decided to write Chapter 2 of her book about her imaginary dog, Fluffy, and Brianne began to add some more specific examples to her tale about a dissatisfied elephant. Matt struggled with his protagonist's quest. They were all absorbed in their work.

Peter, Tom, and Bobby had no idea what they wanted to write about, so I met with them briefly to see if I could spark their interest in a topic. We discussed general categories, and fishing elicited the most interest. I suggested a new strategy—freewriting—and gave them directions to write without stopping for five minutes, with fishing as the theme. They separated reluctantly and I moved on to Yvette. In Yvette's fictional piece a girl has come to live with the narrator and her family. I had already questioned her about the visitor: What makes Lisa Merrie different? How does she fit into the family? Last night, Yvette struggled to answer these questions, so she was anxious to have some time with me. Then Grant wanted to talk with me about his scary butcher story, because previously I had pushed him to show rather than tell that the mild-mannered butcher had suddenly been transformed into a monster. Not an easy task for a ten-year-old, I know, so I was prepared to use some examples as models.

I looked around the classroom. I saw Dana alone and went to work with her. Dana's problems with spelling have made her a reluctant writer. When I conferred with her I focused on her ideas and the design of her story first. I always worked with her spelling, too, to help her become more confident. I also stopped by to talk with shy Nicole and to offer encouragement. She wanted to tell me about her piece, so I listened, told her something I liked about her writing, and asked a question for her to consider as she worked on her next draft. The one-on-one, writer-to-writer interaction keeps me in touch with each child's actual process of writing. I reinforce strategies I have taught in our mini-lessons. I give encouragement. And I listen so that writers will hear and discover for themselves where the power or the problem lies. Writers need time to share their writing.

Because I move from person to person, I am in charge of the tempo of the classroom. As the writers attack their individual projects, I seek out those who have told me they'd like to confer and those I've decided need some teacher time. I control the length of these conferences, too, so that I might meet with many children in one day. And I strive for brevity so that the child's responsibility for the writing isn't compromised by an overeager teacher.

With ten minutes left, it was time for group share. We gathered on the rug and listened as Andreas shared his fable about dolphins. Group share gives writers a larger audience and provides feedback for revision. It also helps writers grow in confidence as we share our writing again and again. Occasionally I read my own writing to the children, which helps them see the process at work in an adult's experience. Their responses compel me to revise, and they begin to understand how a writer can struggle for just the right word or decide to delete whole paragraphs to make the meaning more precise. Kids know that I don't just talk about writing: I write.

The ultimate group share is our authors' day celebration, when each writer takes a turn in the author's chair and listeners write personal responses to the authors. Lauren glowed as she clutched the valued copy of her story in one hand and the jotted notes from her peers in the other. She knew that she is indeed a writer. I treasure these experiences as I join the enthusiastic applause when everyone is finished.

When I was a girl, Friday was spelling test day. Everyone could count on it. Ten words or twenty, sometimes fifty. Monday through Thursday we'd plod our way through the spelling workbook, writing the words ten times each, using them in sentences, seeing the patterns in the word lists. Mrs. Morris would dictate them, carefully pausing between words. Sometimes she'd put the word in a sentence, sometimes not. I still remember learning to spell *appreciate* for her. It seemed like such a big word for a third grader. She recorded our successes on a chart, but everyone's performance was not commendable. So while Elizabeth always got a gold star for her 100, and Daniel, Shannon, Jeff, and I mostly did, many of my friends had few or no stars after their names. Only the perfect spelling papers with excellent handwriting went up on the bulletin board.

In my classroom spelling becomes a key issue when we discuss publishing. My aim throughout the year is to have the children constantly publishing their writing. They may produce classroom anthologies of stories or poems; their pieces might be selected for the Author of the Month bulletin board in the main corridor of the school; they may respond with keen interest to the contests that I announce and post or to professional publications that solicit children's writing. Other bulletin boards in the corridor and classroom also display children's writing. In every case I expect that this writing will be free of spelling and grammatical errors, and I ask kids to do a number of things: keep a list of their personal spelling demons, ask a good speller for assistance, circle words they think are misspelled and look them up in the dictionary, and finally, turn in their final copy to the editor, me, for proofreading. They still miss some words, so I point them out and they transfer them to their spelling demons list for future work. Fifth graders consistently miss the *their/there/they're* trio and the *your/you're* and *it's/its* pairs, so I conduct small-group lessons on ways to master these words and hold the children accountable for using them correctly. Accepting responsibility and knowing that spelling counts are essential in my classroom.

As I work in my classroom, my own childhood memories influence me. I am the teacher I am because of and in spite of the ways in which I was taught. (My mother would be surprised to learn that I rarely use a red pencil and hardly ever write on kids' papers.) When I look back at my elementary school days, I distinctly remember wondering what it was like for kids who didn't learn as quickly as some of the rest of us, pondering how the teacher could have made learning more interesting, and vowing I'd be different. Yet for many years I struggled to find my child's voice in the teacher's role, and my early teaching was often based on my own childhood, adolescent, and college models.

Now that I have begun to change, I've become aware of how difficult it is for parents who were taught one way to have their own children taught differently. Even trying to explain it to my husband has been hard. But an experience this past Thanksgiving helped me understand why I feel so strongly about who I am now and why I do what I do.

My husband thought that this year for Thanksgiving we should have *Gourmet* magazine's sweet potato cloverleaf rolls and that I should make them. His suggestion—and confidence in me—was a bit overwhelming. I am a bread baker and have mastered many simple recipes as well as fancy ones, but I had never attempted rolls before or used anything like mashed sweet potatoes in my bread baking. Always open to new challenges, however, I read the recipe, gathered the ingredients together, and waited for Thanksgiving morning.

After stuffing the turkey, I began the rolls. Bread baking with yeast takes time. After setting the yeast to work, measuring the flour, and mixing the sweet potatoes, eggs, and sugar with the other ingredients, I was finally ready to knead. And as I worked that orangey sweet dough with my hands, I began to think about why I knew I could make these rolls. All my experience as a bread baker gave me the confidence to try this new and unusual recipe.

In my reverie I realized that this self-assurance was what I give my students by immersing them in literature and writing experiences. As a novice bread baker I had read books about the art of bread baking, had considered bread-baking classes, and knew there were Julia Child videos available. But I really learned to bake bread by making it—by testing the temperature, by watching the yeast grow, by feeling the dough under my hands. With practice I knew when to add more flour, when to punch the dough down and let it rise again. My experience led me to try new recipes.

In bread baking you can't separate out the skills, one by one, to practice them; it's the whole process that counts—the fresh ingredients, the accurate temperature, the careful measuring, the steady kneading, the slow rising. So, too, with learning. The steps are all there, to be sure, and each learner needs to experience them over and over again. The old maxim is true: practice makes perfect, but not practice only in proofing yeast. It's the whole experience that makes a reader and a writer. We learn by engaging in the whole process. As a teacher, I need to remember this so that, just as my family and friends savored the light, melt-in-your-mouth rolls with our Thanksgiving dinner, my students can savor the accomplishment of real communication of their own ideas and feelings.

I will work hard this year with your child. We'll read and write every day. We'll share our ideas with each other in our language laboratory, and we'll tackle new tasks as we learn from one another. There's a whole world to read and write about. I'm anxious to know you, too, so that you can work with me to make this a wonderful year for your child. After all, we've got the ingredients, I've rolled up my sleeves, and now it's time to bake the bread.

Sincerely,
Linda Hughs

References

Avi. 1977. *Captain Grey*. New York: Pantheon Books.
———. 1981. *A Place Called Ugly*. New York: Pantheon Books.
———. 1984. *The Fighting Ground*. New York: J. B. Lippincott.

A LETTER TO PARENTS ABOUT INVENTED SPELLING

MARY ELLEN GIACOBBE
Atkinson, New Hampshire

When I first started teaching, in the early seventies, my daughter Gale's kindergarten teacher informed me that Gale didn't know all the letters and sounds. Since I'd never done any letter/phonics drills with her, I thought that maybe it was my fault, and I wondered if she needed one of those plaid phonics workbooks. Her teacher proceeded to show me a booklet she had confiscated from Gale. She wanted Gale to stop "playing" writing until she knew her letters and sounds. The colorfully illustrated four-page story, with cover and "the end" page, went like this (Gale's version is at the left):

the flwr and the wrm	The Flower and the Worm
It wz the Ant's brfday	It was the ant's birthday.
tha had cakc and iskren	They had cake and ice cream
and big presints sea the flwr	and big presents. See the flower.
the elafint wz havn a	The elephant was having a
good tim splachen wotr	good time splashing water.
the ENd	The end

When I read the story I was amazed and proud. I laughed at the animals having a birthday party and the elephant splashing everyone and couldn't believe I could read every word of it. The stern look on the teacher's face brought me back to reality.

Back then I didn't know how to respond when the teacher focused on what Gale couldn't do as a writer. Now as I look at this piece of writing I marvel at all the things she *could* do. She knew that stories have titles. She put one idea about the party on each page. Her illustrations matched her text. Her knowledge about phonics and how to write words was revealed in many ways:

1. She used sixteen of the twenty-one consonant sounds correctly: *b, c, d, f, g, h, k, l, m, n, r, s, t, v, w, z* (although *f* doesn't occur in "birthday," she pronounced it "birfday").
2. She used three vowels correctly, both long and short *a, e,* and *i.*
3. She used *fl, ay, th, pr,* and *spl* correctly.
4. She used eight sight words: *it, the, had, and, big, a, good, end.*
5. She used apostrophe *s* to show possession (*ant's*).

Through playing with letters and sounds, Gale was learning how to express herself. Although I can look at this piece of writing now with respect for the amount of hard work that went into it, I'm sorry I was unaware of it then. Charles Read had conducted groundbreaking research on young children and their phonology, but his findings hadn't yet been reported in the most widely read teacher's journals (1970, 1971). Carol Chomsky's work on invented spelling had also been published but in journals I wasn't aware of at the time (1970, 1971a, 1971b). Their research demonstrated that Gale was participating in written language as best she knew how, and that her invented spelling, sometimes called *temporary spelling,* actually revealed her complex thinking about how to use letters and sounds to communicate with others.

When Donald Graves, Susan Sowers, and Lucy Calkins came into my first-grade classroom in 1978 to conduct their two-year study of children's writing, they helped me begin to focus on what my students *could* do. In order to make sense of my observations, I read the research of Read, Chomsky, and Glenda Bissex (1980). I learned that all children can write and that I must value their temporary spellings as clues to their thinking. Their inventions are windows on their minds—a way they reveal their thinking about how our language works. And I learned that parents need help in understanding their child's attempts so that they, too, can see through the window and marvel with us. If we as teachers don't let parents in on what we do, they will be confused by invented spelling. They may worry about our apparent disregard for correct spelling. They may see mistakes go uncorrected and believe that we are encouraging poor spelling habits. Worst of all, some parents may suspect that teachers themselves do not know how to spell correctly.

The following letter is one that primary teachers might wish to consider as they explain what their students are doing and how parents can participate in children's emerging literacy. It is the letter I wish my daughter's kindergarten teacher had sent me.

Dear Parents,

Since the first day of school, your child has participated in our writer's workshop, a time when the children are encouraged to write about something they know about. As they started telling their stories, I was amazed at all the things your children know and the rich language they use to talk about their knowledge. Their topics included horseback riding lessons, losing a first tooth, a twin brother, a boat ride, going to the hospital, a Christmas party, Grandma, Cape Cod, Disneyworld, treehouses, and skating.

Through both drawings and words the children expressed their ideas on paper. When I introduced the writer's workshop to them, I showed them a way they could write independently without my assistance. I modeled how I say a word slowly, listen carefully to the sounds I hear, and then write a letter to represent each sound. I asked, "If you want to write *volcano*, say the word slowly, and what do you hear?" The children heard V-L-K-N-O. This spelling of *volcano* is called an *invented* or *temporary* spelling. This close approximation of the spelling of *volcano* is what the children are able to do for now. Figure 1 (page 28) shows an example of Joseph's writing from the first day's workshop.

Joseph has done a lot of hard work. His piece helps me to understand what he already knows about written language:

1. He knows that he can express his ideas through drawing and words and that the drawing and the words go together.
2. He knows that writing moves in a left-to-right direction.
3. He knows that when he comes to the end of a line, he needs to go to the beginning of the next line and once again write from left to right.
4. He hears individual sounds when he says words.
5. He knows that sounds are represented by letters.
6. He uses eight consonants: *m, f, r, n, t, h, d,* and *k*.
7. He uses two long vowels: *i* and *e*.

Most important, he knows that he has a subject worth writing about and that he is a writer.

When Joseph showed me his drawing and read his writing to me, we talked about his dad fishing and not catching anything

Figure 1   Joseph's writing: "My father [was] fishing in the water. He didn't catch any fish."

and how frustrating that must have been. I also asked, "What was the problem?"

He replied, "I don't know . . . there were all kinds of fish swimming around." At that point, he picked up his crayon and drew seven fish in the water.

As I talked to Joseph, my concern was with the meaning of his story and trying to understand it better. Then, when I talked to him about how he wrote down his words, I acknowledged what he knew how to do: "When you said *my*, you heard *m* and you wrote an *M* to represent that sound." I did not correct his temporary spellings at this time because this beginning writer needs lots of opportunities to try his best and have his efforts valued and accepted. Over time I will build upon his attempts and work with him toward conventional spelling.

I wasn't always so understanding. Before I began to look into the research on how children learn to write, I corrected everything. Furthermore, I believed that in order to write, first graders would first have to know all the letters and their sounds and how to read. I was wrong.

Research helped me to see that learning to write is like learning to talk. When your children first began to talk, you didn't insist on correct pronunciation. You didn't drill them on isolated sounds. You didn't provide the kinds of school lessons we were accustomed to in our school days. Instead, the first time your children said, "mmm," you were sure they were saying *mama*. You were excited and you encouraged them to say it over and over again. (And need I remind you that in some instances you might even have encouraged an unconventional, wrong pronunciation?) Because your children were surrounded by the speech of parents, siblings, relatives, friends, radio, television, repairwomen, salesmen, and many others, they heard *mom* and, through a lot of play and experimentation, they eventually said *mom*, too. Their early invented talking, or temporary talking, did not alarm you or cause you to send them to a remedial talking class. You accepted these early approximations. Your children learned to talk by talking in a supportive environment with people who believed they had something worth saying.

I apply the same model children used when they acquired oral language to help them acquire written language. The classroom is a literate environment filled with opportunities to use language in all its forms—talking, listening, reading, and writing. When children write they use the rich oral language they learned at home before they came to school. By providing opportunities for children to use temporary spellings, I encourage them to spell words based upon what they can do. They formulate their own rules about our spelling system. I know my adult standards of correctness are not appropriate for beginning writers.

My beginning writers need time, too. I know how discouraging it is for them to feel pressured to spell words *right*. When children must spell correctly, they are limited in what they can write. They use safe words and write things like "I love my cat. I love my dog. I love mom. I love dad," instead of "My cat got sec and wey hand to taeyc hrey to the vatnnearnary" (My cat got sick and we had to take her to the veterinary). As time goes on, when we have editing conferences, I will build upon their knowledge and help them take another step toward conventional spelling. For example, Mary wrote what's shown in Figure 2 (page 30). After we talked about the rides at the fair and further developed the meaning of her story, I pointed out to Mary what she can do as a writer:

1. In addition to all the things Joseph demonstrated in his piece of writing, she has a sense of word, since she leaves spaces between words.
2. She knows seven sight words: *I, went, to, a, and, but, them.*
3. She is aware of punctuation and uses a period to designate the end of a sentence.
4. She has developed a temporary rule for when she hears long *e* at the end of a word: she uses *i* as in *veri, veri, skari*. Since her name has a long *e* sound at the end, represented by *y*, this is something I clarified for her during our conference.
5. Since Mary is a reader, it's my hunch that she has seen *e* at the end of words and knows it has no sound. She's not sure what to do with the *e*, but she knows some words have it, so she's experimenting (*fare, ridse, relaksinge*). Silent *e* at the end of a word is something else we talked about.

Figure 2   Mary's writing: "I went to a fair and there was very, very scary rides but some of them were very relaxing."

The individual conference is one way in which I build upon what children know and help them take another step. I also meet with the whole class at the beginning of each writer's workshop for a brief lesson and present information about the qualities of good writing, how writers practice their craft, and the skills they need to know.

Periodically, I'll publish some of their writings—that is, I'll be their editor and type their works in a conventional form with correct spelling and punctuation. These published pieces of writing will be placed in our classroom library and become part of our reading program. In time, as the children become more experienced writers, they will take more and more responsibility for their own proofreading and editing.

Why do I provide time for your children to write every day in the way I've described? Through the years I've learned that when I encourage children to take the risks necessary to write, they become confident, competent writers. They learn how to create texts that readers can understand, enjoy, and learn from. And in another letter, I'll discuss with you how it affects them as readers.

Parents often ask what they can do to help their children as they begin to learn to write. When your children ask, "How do you spell ———?", encourage them by saying, "What do you hear?" or "What do you think?" In other words, your children need you to support their attempts—their thinking—as you did when they learned to speak. Remember, too, to talk with your children about what you enjoy and understand about their writing and to help them see what they *can* do.

I'm encouraged by the early writing of your children and can't wait to publish some of their stories to share with all of you.

Sincerely,
Mary Ellen Giacobbe

References

Bissex, Glenda. 1980. *GNYS AT WRK: A Child Learns to Write and Read.* Cambridge, MA: Harvard University Press.

Chomsky, Carol. 1970. "Reading, Writing, and Phonology." *Harvard Educational Review* 40:287–309.

———. 1971a. "Write First, Read Later." *Childhood Education* 47:296–99.

———. 1971b. "Invented Spelling in the Open Classroom." *Word* 27:1–3.

Read, Charles. 1970. "Children's Perceptions of the Sounds of English: Phonology from Three to Six." Doctoral dissertation, Harvard University.

———. 1971. "Pre-school Children's Knowledge of English Phonology." *Harvard Educational Review* 41:1–34.

An Author's Perspective
THE KOALA AS A TEACHER
OF READING

I'm suffering a series of passions at the moment: a bother over the struggle for a definition of "whole language," a misery over the lack of trust we have in learners, and a horrified astonishment over what's happening to my books in so-called "whole language" classrooms. My aim here is simply to unburden myself. A trouble shared is a trouble halved.

Whole language is the current educational vogue in Australia and New Zealand, and it's fast becoming the fashion in the States as well. However, it's pointless to declare that we're *for* whole language if we don't know what we're *against*. When pressed, I guess we'd have to say that if we're for "wholes" we must be against "parts," but we don't give a lot of thought to this conundrum. That's our first mistake. If we don't comprehend the meaning of "parts"—and my hunch is that many of us don't—how can we begin to understand the meaning of teaching language in "wholes"?

There are those who think whole language means using Big Books in the classroom. Others claim that whole language means literature-based reading. Neither of these beliefs is wholly correct, and many other misconceptions abound. In attempting to head off the chaos, might I suggest that we begin by dropping the term *whole language* without delay? It has given rise to many a molehill and mountain of misunderstanding because its meaning is not explicit. Whole language developed as a counteractive slogan to signpost a new way of teaching language arts in relation to an old way of teaching language arts: that is, wholes versus parts, or to put it more simply, real versus unreal language.

The term *real language* is explicit. Real language isn't a vogue that can be discarded in years to come. We use real language whenever we speak, write, read, or listen. We always have and we always will. We hear real sentences with real meanings in whole conversations. We read real paragraphs in whole books. We write whole words in real notes. We speak real sentences with whole messages. Whole language is nothing more, or less, than real language.

For example, when my husband and I arrive home after work he says to me, "Like a coffee?" It's a message that travels down the real language road in our kitchen from him to me. I respond by relaying a message down the same real language road. "Yes, please," I say. The sentences may be short, but they're definitely real.

Every day I receive many examples of whole language in letters from children who send me bright messages along real language roads that stretch perhaps from the Crocodile Dundee country of Northern Australia right down to my front door: "Mem Fox I love your books. I think you must be a really intelligent woman." A little while later a message goes back: "Thanks a million for your great letter. I'm thrilled you think I'm intelligent. You're intelligent too. You must be: you love my books!!!" These are real messages from a real child to a real author and back again.

Outside educational institutions it's difficult to find language that *isn't* real: from advertisements to blockbuster novels, from parents yelling at kids to lovers whispering on park benches, from doctors' prescriptions to banners on marches, from hymns to rock music, and from articles in *Playboy* to Harvard Ph.D. theses—all traveling along the real language road, carrying meaningful messages from one place to another.

But what do we find inside educational institutions? Many meaningless messages, most often in the form of dead-end ditto-sheets. Figure 1 shows one that was developed, much to my horror, out of one of my books. In some classrooms this travesty passes for "writing." But it's unreal. It's parts of sentences only, not whole sentences. No one in real life fills in ditto-sheets. They are the cul-de-sacs and one-way streets of writing, in which there is no one waiting to receive the message at the end of the road, or wanting to receive it, because it's pointless.

To what extent is literacy achieved, I wonder, through the avalanche of published "part-language" materials such as these? It's my suspicion that educational publishers might have to bear

Figure 1

Hattie and the Fox

Mem Fox   Patricia Mullins

What did they say???

"	!" said Hattie.
"	!" said the goose.
"	!" said the pig.
"	?" said the sheep.
"	?" said the horse.
"	?" said the cow.

Draw the fox jumping from the bushes.

some of the blame for the frightening fact (which I read this year in an airline magazine) that the public schools of this great American nation graduate 700,000 functionally illiterate students per year, while another 700,000 drop out (Kearns and Doyle 1990).

If the writing students use inside the classroom isn't the writing they're going to use outside the classroom, we are wasting time. By spending hours on ditto-sheet activity we produce people who can't write a complete sentence correctly, let alone a paragraph, let alone a lengthy and significant piece of written communication, because we haven't allowed them the time to do it. We haven't provided real reasons to write (or read) real messages that travel down the real language road to (and from) real destinations.

In real life we don't have to engage in inane ditto-sheet activities whenever we read a book. Nor do we have to answer unreal questions on any book we might have read other than "What's it about?" and "Did you enjoy it?" No one asks, thank goodness, if I can remember the names of the social climbers in *Bonfire of the Vanities*. I can't. Who cares anyway? I loved the book. It provided endless fascinating messages along the real language road into my mind and memory. After I'd read it I couldn't stop talking about it. That's whole language. That's a real reaction to a book.

The books children read in class are not always as real as *Hattie and the Fox*, let alone *Bonfire of the Vanities*. For some peculiar reason there's a belief abroad that children have to learn to read by reading unreal books before they're allowed to read real ones. In these basal readers the language is so unnatural it would be funny if it weren't so tragic:

> "Today is Saturday," said Dick.
> "Yes, it is Saturday," said Dora, "so we do not go to school."
> "There is no school on Saturdays," said Mother.
> "Jack and May will not be at school. They will be at home."
> "Fluff and Nip do not go to school at all," said Dora.
> "They stop at home and play."
> "They stop at home and go to sleep," said Dick.
> "Look, Nip is asleep now. Can you see him asleep, Mother?"

No real person would write or speak such boring banalities in such consciously chosen monosyllables. The real language road is not traveled in such a book, with the result that no one in real life reads basals for pleasure. They provide only part of the reason for reading: words.

Basal readers are emotional deserts between two covers. Little children who struggle across the arid vocabulary toward an elusive literacy often collapse along the way, thirsting for the language of life. They find themselves instead surrounded by death: a dead plot here, a dead theme there; a dead tone, dead setting, dead character—everywhere a dead style. How *paltry* to use a book, or to write a book—any book—to teach merely the mechanics of reading. Real books offer a "whole" lot more. They offer the emotional and intellectual mechanics of life itself, along a real language road.

Before we teach children to read we shouldn't ask *how* we're going to do it, but *why*. The "how" can be answered with "basals." But children exposed only to basals must wonder why they should bother to learn to read when reading provides so little pleasure or fascination. There's no impetus to read when the rewards are few. On the other hand, real books—that is, "trade" books—give children many answers to the question "Why read?" They're fun, they're beautiful, they arouse the emotions, they provide information, and they're entertaining—just as entertaining as television.

Basals aggravate the problem of the functionally illiterate because, frankly, they appear to have been written by the functionally illiterate. Johnny can't read—neither can Jenny—because faced with the dullness of a basal, why on earth would they want to? Basals aren't even well-illustrated: the eye is repulsed even before the heart and mind begin to be repelled.

We mustn't continue to allow educational publishers to believe that we're satisfied with the current standard of basal readers. We are *not* satisfied with their dispirited texts written in back rooms by tired hired hacks who think that four-syllable words like *invisible* are too much for a five-year-old to cope with when we know that the opposite is true. But if we continue to seethe in silence, publishers will have every reason to think that we are happy with their products. We'll have only ourselves to blame for the poor materials we're given. It's a supply and demand sitiuation, so let's make new demands. Most of us grumble in vain, in isolation, expecting publishers to be able to read our minds. They can't. But a few million letters might do the trick.

Another peculiarity often found alongside basal readers in a "part-language" classroom is a series of large cards. As the solitary words on these cards are flashed before children's eyes, the children call them out in unison. But to reiterate: words are only parts. They don't work on their own. If my car were pulled to pieces I'd be able to recognize and name the windshield wipers, the seats, the steering wheel, the engine, the clutch, the tires, and so on, but the car wouldn't go no matter how clever I was in naming its parts. It would have to be put together before it was of any use to me. So it is with the words children know in isolation. They're useless unless they're connected in a meaningful whole sentence, paragraph, letter, advertisement, story, joke, or similarly real language transaction—in order to arrive at a real place along the real language road.

For this reason also I'm also deeply suspicious of spelling competitions. Spelling correctly is extremely important, I don't deny, but being able to spell unconnected words, for no real language reason, seems to me to be just plain silly. A waste of time, all these "parts." They prove nothing. On the other hand, the ability to spell words correctly in a real letter to a real president, for example, about a real issue like the homeless, would not only be admirable, it would be essential. A real letter to the president! And a real reply expected! What a prime exhibit of whole language at work.

As distasteful as spelling competitions, to my way of thinking, are the spurious schemes—such as read-a-thons—run by fast-food outlets and other well-meaning organizations, which encourage children to read by offering them extrinsic rewards for having read so many books. This is not whole language because it's not real. The intrinsic joy of reading is demeaned and devalued by these bumbling do-gooders. Their subtle but very damaging message is: "Hey, look, kids! We know reading is a real drag but we've got a great little something for you if you can just grit your teeth and knuckle down to reading a few lousy books." Such schemes have no place in genuine whole language classrooms.

It's easy to be fooled into thinking that something whole must also be real. Incredible though it may seem, it is possible in a "part-language" school to discover a child actually writing a *whole* letter—say, an application for a job. But it's not real because at the end of the lesson the letter isn't posted; it's given to a teacher who will grade it and give it back. This is a perfect example of the language road reaching a dead end. Any writing written for no one, for no reason, for no response, which is filed away on completion in a desk or a folder is surely pointless. Writers only care about writing well when they care about the outcome of what they have written. A "pretend" job application, like a pretend anything, has no consequence attached to it. Where there's no consequence there is no real engagement by the writer; where there's no engagement there's no improvement in the writing.

Perhaps we've forgotten to trust our own judgment. Under an external hail of instructions and material, excellent teachers—and I include myself among them, immodestly!—have lost confidence in the value of their own common sense. Many of us have been conditioned into believing that only the experts have answers and that we aren't the experts.

Yet we are experts. It's easy for us to compare our personal use of language with our teaching use of language and shudder if the two don't match up. And then change our ways. For example, if we ask ourselves what we write and why, and when and how we write, we might be shocked to discover that in the classroom we are asking children to engage in the very activities we'd hate to do ourselves, such as ripping literature into a million different parts for dead-end written analysis of one kind or another, tossing it into ditches beside the real language road, and never putting it back together again in complete, coherent, and enjoyable wholes for the forgotten prime purposes of entertainment and information.

Similarly, if we ask ourselves what we read and why, and when and how we read, we might be just as shocked to discover for a second time that our classroom methods are far removed from our own real-life habits. Would we read, I wonder, if we had to stand up and read aloud, all alone, a book chosen by someone else to an uninterested person sitting at a desk? No wonder one small girl said, "I hate reading. My legs get tired." Would we read if, at the end of each novel, we had to write a book review, or a different ending, or a list of ten adjectives describing the main character? A trade book publisher in Australia supplies these vile, going-nowhere suggestions to "enhance" the teaching of its superb books. The books are gold, the suggested activities filth.

Would we look forward to reading, or bother to read at all, if we had to keep an ongoing journal of our feelings and reactions *during* the reading of that novel? Wouldn't that slow us down considerably? Wouldn't becoming a writing-reader interfere markedly with being a reading-reader, lost in another world created by an author who has written specifically to engage our undivided attention? Might it not be a touch insulting to authors to drive an unnatural wedge between their texts and their readers? A post-novel-reading reaction (which may be very useful and even popular, depending on the creative nature of the assignment) is surely a better way of doing things, but in any case, who would want to write one after every book she'd read? Not me.

Why are we so lacking in trust that we can't allow a good book to teach its own reading? And why do we underestimate the brainpower of our students to such an extent that we believe, as one educationally half-witted publisher does, that Katherine Paterson's exquisite *Bridge to Terabithia* needs to appear in an abridged version? Abridged! Heavens, it's not nineteenth-century Jane Austen! It's not even Harriet Beecher Stowe. Who would want parts of any Katherine Paterson novel if they could have the whole book? Why do intelligent people, like publishers, parents, and teachers, expect so little literacy from their intelligent, bright, inquisitive children? Why aim for the mud when we can aim for the stars? If we continue to slide in our expectations, the rest of the world will pass us by and in time we'll come to believe that Dr. Seuss is too difficult for doctoral students.

When I write for children I forget the notion of difficulty. I concentrate instead on joy and passion. My readers and listeners range from babies to senior citizens. All I want from them at the end of one of my stories is a sigh of contentment because they have shared a passionate experience with me. (Such a sigh has never yet been heard at the end of a basal reader.) The sigh is important. It's a signal from children that reading or listening to literature has been rewarding. It points to the possibility in children's minds that reading might be rewarding again and again.

The shared experience in my books isn't necessarily pleasant, even though my characters usually smile on the last page. In *Wilfrid Gordon McDonald Partridge*, Miss Nancy loses her memory. In *Koala Lou* an important competition is lost and Koala Lou howls her eyes out. In *Night Noises* a child could be scared half to death before reaching the playful denouement. In *Guess What?* Daisy O'Grady is utterly revolting and the pictures are enough to make a child's hair stand on end. And in *Hattie and the Fox* the farmyard animals are not in the happiest of situations vis-à-vis the fox.

The common element in these stories is that they don't put a pretty face on real life. I'm all for reality in the home, not only along the language arts road or in the whole language classroom, since kids live in a real world and must face a series of real challenges every day. Life isn't all sugar—there's a lot of vinegar as well. By denying the vinegar in literature we provide bland, inoffensive, unappealing lies to children who know the truth. Lies don't make good reading. Lies don't invite young readers inside the cover of another book, and another. (Basals, of course, tell the biggest lies of all.) Why don't we trust children to cope with the sad and the bad? Why do we underestimate their capabilities at *every* age?

In my most recent about-to-be-published story, *Ben Times Two*, a boy, Johnno, temporarily loses his father, Ben, as the result of a divorce. I don't use the word *divorce*, but the situation is unambiguous. Johnno and his mother buy a puppy to cheer themselves up. Early in the story the following conversation ensues:

> "What will we call him?" asked Johnno.
> "You choose," said his mother.
> Johnno thought for a while.
> "Let's call him Ben," he said at last.
> Ben was the name of his father.
> "All right," said his mother, in a tight voice.

An editor wanted me to remove "in a tight voice." She thought it made the mother sound angry. Good grief! Must we now pretend that mothers are all sugar and no vinegar? That they are never angry or upset? I pointed out that the mother *was* angry. The phrase was retained. It tells a truth that catches at people's hearts. It might therefore "catch" readers at the same time, without ditto-sheets, without unnecessary questions on what kind of dog Ben was, without rewriting the ending (my teeth are grinding at the thought), and without presenting a reluctant, lackluster book review.

I'm a great believer in the power of passion to get kids hooked on books, so I always hope teachers will allow my books to stand alone for what they are, for they what say, and for what they contribute to the natural, joyful development of children's literacy. I'm a teacher too, after all, and I weave a million little teaching points in and out of the passion of my stories to exterminate the need for any nasty "part-language" activities that some educational demolitionist might dream up.

In *Koala Lou*, for instance, there's a recurring endearment from mother to child: "Koala Lou, I DO love you!" It's passion, certainly, but the constant repetition of that line on page after page teaches children eventually to recognize the words through an emotional attachment to literature. It's "whole" language with a meaningful connection to real life. The koala, if we dare to leave her alone, is an excellent teacher of reading.

I employed the same technique of repetition, but less obviously, in *Wilfrid Gordon*. The line "What's a memory?" occurs five times, making it five times easier to read than if it had occurred only once. The elderly people reply five times, using the same construction but a different term of address:

Something warm, my child, something warm.
Something from long ago, me lad, something from long ago.
Something that makes you cry, my boy, something that makes you cry.

And so on. Each sentence is only half as difficult to read as it might have been, since the first phrase is mirrored by the last—and kids soon cotton on to that.

My books just happen to have rhyme, rhythm, and repetition in them because it's second nature for me as a writer to know what's required for young readers. I'm aware that I accidentally teach reading through the arrangement of my structures, sentences, and words, but my first intention, always, is to produce (if I can!) an irresistible work of art. Irresistible works of art, if we dare to leave them alone, are excellent teachers of reading.

They are also excellent teachers of writing. From studying myself as a writer, as well as my extended family (several of whom are writers), and from thousands of examples of student writers in over twenty years of teaching, I've come to the conclusion that wide reading is the only effective way of learning how to write well. It's true that there are certain hints teachers can offer in so-called creative writing classes, such as the basic mechanics, the need to draft, the importance of leads, how to show not tell, and why adjectives might not be such a good idea after all, but the deep elements of style can only be grasped, I believe, after long exposure to the best that literature has to offer. I'm aware that this exposure to fine language and elegant style has to start with me, in my own books for little children. It's a frightening responsibility. I can't afford the time to write down to children. The race is on: I must write up.

I tried to do just that, and I hope I succeeded, in *Night Noises*. The similes on the second page introduce a way of painting with words that children might not have come across before: "Her hair was as wispy as cobwebs in ceilings. Her bones were as creaky as floorboards at midnight." The similes also set the tone of a dark-and-stormy-night story. In the natural learning environment, in which the story might be read half a dozen times in as many weeks, the words and structures will be stored away in the minds of the listeners until they're needed for writing or speaking, perhaps fifty years later.

Also provided—inadvertently—in *Night Noises* is a regular little thesaurus in bold red lettering. As the excitement mounts outside old Lily Laceby's cottage, large red words heighten the tension: "MURMUR MUTTER SHHHH; SQUINT PEEK PEER; TWIST TEST RATTLE; YELL CLATTER BANG BANG BANG." Writers of basal readers wouldn't countenance the inclusion of a "difficult" word like *squint* in a book aimed at five-year-olds, because they underestimate children's needs and abilities as well as their capacity to enjoy words for words' sake. How can children write with a sharply focused clarity if they don't know words with different shades of meaning? *Peer* is as qualitatively different from *squint* as yellow is from orange. Imagine being restricted to one shade of yellow when there's a setting sun to be painted! There's a great deal of power in the ability to use words with precision, but there's not much power to be dragged from the words in a basal reader.

It seems obvious that the answer is to provide children with beautiful books, written by real, well-known writers for real live kids, whose real live intelligence will be not be underestimated. In theory, teaching reading with real literature ought to be successful. Mostly it is. It is the method used in Australia and New Zealand, both of which have a high rate of literacy in comparison to Great Britain and the United States. Tragically, however, even in Australia there exist teachers who have jumped onto the unreliable whole language bandwagon without first abandoning parts. They hang onto parts without understanding that the "use by" date has expired.

Recently I received a letter summing up a school project on Mem Fox and her books. In despair I leafed through the pile of material that had been sent to me with so much professional pride. My heart bled for the little souls whose journey along the real language road had been littered with rotten bits of language, such as the ditto on *Wilfrid* shown in Figure 2, and the earlier worksheet on *Hattie*.

Figure 2

Wilfrid Gordon McDonald Partridge

Mem Fox   Julie Vivas

Mrs Jordan who
_____

Mr. Hosking who
_____

Mr. Tippet who
_____

Miss Mitchell who
_____

Mr. Drysdale who
_____

Miss Nancy who
_____

Who lost her memory?
_____

How old was Miss Nancy?
_____

Draw Wilfrid's memory objects:
Shells   Puppet   Medal   Football   Egg

Parents trust children to learn to talk, and without any abnormal speaking practice or pointless exercises they learn how to talk. Why does trust in learners disappear when they leave home and "progress" to school? The worksheets based on my books upset me for several reasons:

- They demonstrated a lack of trust in the books to do their own work.
- They bored children who had only just been hooked into books.
- There was no real communicative reason to write—that is, no meaning was passed from one person to another along a real language road.
- In *Hattie and the Fox*, the recurrent line on each page is "And Hattie said, 'Goodness gracious me!' " but the worksheet required the sentence to read " 'Goodness gracious me!' said Hattie," thereby causing confusion and probably undoing any joyful repetitive learning that had already taken place.
- The age of Miss Nancy was/is immaterial.
- The question "Who lost her memory?" demeaned the children's intelligence.
- The sentences beginning "Mrs. Jordan who . . ." were bad examples of English to set before children, because when the blanks were filled in, as in "Mrs. Jordan, who played the organ," the meaning remained incomplete, in sentences without main verbs.

These exercises stole time from the writing of real English, for real purposes, for real people, for real responses, in spite of the fact that the whole language benefits of the earlier activities were more than sufficient to develop the children's reading and writing, speaking and listening skills. The teachers were well-meaning, but their unwillingness to abandon parts before they embraced wholes revealed a basic ignorance of current beliefs about language learning—an ignorance that retards the teaching of reading and writing and seriously undermines the potential of the whole language approach.

I'm aware that what I have said here casts a certain amount of gloom on the current state of language arts teaching, but I felt it was necessary to define the darkness in order to be able to recognize the light. I had to unburden myself. Or weep.

I'm also aware that I have railed against specific practices without presenting in any detail my own manifesto on the "right" way to teach language and literature. This was deliberate. I didn't want to fall into the trap of sounding like a whole language expert who had the right answers. No one has the right answers. It's more important to have the right questions.

I believe that in order to teach real language successfully, you and I have only to understand the quality of *reality*, through personal observation and reflection, and to nurture its existence in our classrooms. "Is it real? Is it real? Is it real?" should be our daily educational mantra. If it were, and if we took notice of it in our teaching, we'd never again need to jump on anything so humdrum as bandwagons. Instead, we'd be in winged chariots, flying along the real language road toward the brilliant sunrise of universal literacy.

References

Fox, Mem. 1985. *Wilfrid Gordon McDonald Partridge*. Brooklyn, NY: Kane/Miller.

———. 1986. *Hattie and the Fox*. New York: Bradbury Press.

———. 1988a. *Guess What?* New York: Harcourt Brace Jovanovich.

———. 1988b. *Koala Lou*. New York: Harcourt Brace Jovanovich.

———. 1989. *Night Noises*. New York: Harcourt Brace Jovanovich.

Kearns and Doyle. 1990. "Winning the Brain Race." *Spirit: The Magazine of Southwest Arilines* (ICS Press). April.

Paterson, Katherine. 1977. *Bridge to Terabithia*. New York: Harper & Row.

Wolfe, Tom. 1988. *The Bonfire of the Vanities*. New York: Random House.

PORTFOLIOS ACROSS THE CURRICULUM

MARK MILLIKEN
Stratham Memorial School
Stratham, New Hampshire

Gramma said when you come on something good,
first thing to do is share it
with whoever you can find;
that way, the good spreads out where no
telling it will go.
Which is right.

Forrest Carter,
The Education of Little Tree

*M*y fifth-grade class and I came upon something good this year when we started using portfolios across the curriculum in an attempt to involve students and parents in the assessment process. We started with what we knew.

I asked the kids to recall the work they had collected from last year and handed on to me: a writing sample and a list of their five favorite books. We talked about what this sample and list showed about them as learners. Then I wrote "portfolio assessment" on the board and asked what they thought it meant. Very little. Then I asked them to talk with their parents about their thoughts on portfolios, and my students came back the next day with the following information.

Portfolios

- contain something you feel good about
- are very neat
- show some type of an inventory
- depend on what you are working on

Krystal's mother, an interior decorator, volunteered to let us look at one of her portfolios. Ms. Chase kept her portfolio in an impressive black case that zipped closed. It was large and contained pictures, letters, and magazine covers. The kids gathered around our horseshoe table to get as close to it as they could. After plenty of study and discussion we generated a list of what the portfolio showed about Ms. Chase:

- What she works on
- What work she likes best
- Her best examples (samples)
- Newspaper articles about her work

- What kinds of designs she does
- How good she is
- Before and after examples
- Magazine covers showing her work
- Very professional case

We now had a much better idea of what a portfolio was. Ms. Chase's portfolio became the real-life foundation that the class continually referred to when they had questions about how to proceed with their own portfolios. The kids were also excited by the physical appearance of the model. This was the point at which the portfolio concept became theirs. I asked how we could apply this idea to school, and they looked at the list, still on the board, and substituted school-related items: they could show what they were good at, include before and after examples of their writing, and provide information about themselves as readers, mathematicians, and social studies and science students. And so we jumped in, none of us able to predict what the outcome would be. We had two weeks before grades closed for term two.

I drifted around the room that first day, observing the progress, and became worried by the amount of time the class was spending on constructing their portfolios: out came construction paper, scissors, glue, rulers, and tape. The room bustled with excited work, and I had a sinking feeling in my belly. After a good part of the morning had passed in this fashion, I stopped the class and asked how they felt things were going. They had a few questions:

- Are we just evaluated on our best work?
- How do we put math in?
- Can we work on them at home?
- Do we only put in work from term two?
- If it's messy do we have to do it over?
- Can we have before and after examples from term one?

- Can we put our whole social studies log in?
- Do we have to finish today?

Their questions reassured me that they understood portfolios and helped me to guide their course. I like to operate in this manner: to let the class jump in after a little introduction, then to stop and ask what's going well and what they want to work on next. From their questions I knew that although they were still constructing the physical portfolios, their minds were already at work on the contents.

The first question, about evaluation of best work, sparked a discussion of assessment and how people show progress. We also talked about whether Ms. Chase had included only her best work, and they remembered that she did include pictures of work in progress so that we could see her growth.

The question about math referred to the fact that they had done a lot of work with manipulatives. How could they show these in a portfolio? Many students decided to draw pictures and diagrams representing manipulative work, which pleased me because, as my experience shows, going from concrete manipulatives to representational pictures is the natural development of concept attainment. The portfolio concept was already blending with my curriculum.

I wanted the portfolios to stay at school at this time. I had visions of partially assembled portfolios going home and staying home, and students with half their work at home and half at school. I explained this to my students, and they understood.

We addressed the questions that students raised about work from terms one and two by referring to Ms. Chase's example. In order to show a progression of work, an artist compares earlier and current efforts. In my classroom the kids save all of their work: a file cabinet contains two drawers devoted to student files, which are managed by the students themselves. These include math folders, which hold any loose papers and tests, spelling folders, folders for drafts of writing they are no longer working on, and, as the year progressed and we worked with portfolios more, folders for any material they no longer wished to include in their current portfolios.

My students also do a lot of thinking, writing, and experimenting in academic journals or learning logs. Each student has a log for each subject, and these are another great resource for demonstrating progress. They wondered how to represent this work in their portfolios; some asked if they could include the whole log. Once again we talked about Ms. Chase's portfolio and discussed whether or not she showed all of her work. We concluded that she decided which work would best represent her abilities, and this was what my students did with their logs: they rewrote or photocopied their best log entries for inclusion in the portfolios.

My favorite question was "Do we have to finish today?" because it showed how new the concept was. Portfolios take so much time and thought, contain so much information, and yield so many insights, that putting one together would take much longer than a day.

Kinds of Portfolios

The physical portfolios—the cases—fell into five categories: handmade nonfunctional, handmade functional, loose-leaf notebook, trapper keeper, and photo album. The first time we used portfolios there were many handmade varieties; by the end of the year most students were using one of the three other options.

The first category of portfolios looked almost exactly like Ms. Chase's portfolio. Made of construction paper with black covers, they even had little black handles. I termed them nonfunctional because every piece of work represented in them had to be pasted onto construction paper pages and could only be used once. Our goal was to have ongoing portfolios that changed as the learner changed. The process the kids went through in thinking about and developing the portfolio case was much like the thinking that goes on in the first drafts of writing. Next year I will stipulate that whatever format they use must be functional, that is, able to grow and change.

Some handmade portfolios were functional. They had pages with construction paper pockets for each subject, which allowed papers to be taken out or added. There were a few drawbacks here: the pockets turned out to be narrower than regular-sized paper, so students had to trim their papers with scissors. The portfolios also deteriorated with each use—something I did not have to point out as some students started using other, sturdier types of cases. An unexpected offshoot of using portfolios was an improvement in students' organizational habits. Parents also noticed this and commented positively about it.

Trapper keepers became a popular alternative. We even noticed that the pocketed folders came with the word *portfolio* printed on them. This kind of notebook helped a number of my students organize themselves because each subject could have a separate folder.

Amber's reading folder exemplifies how the trapper keeper worked. On one side she included a reading log entry she had chosen to represent herself as a reader for the term. In the other pocket of the folder she inserted each term's reading list—a record of all the books she had read, including the author, number of pages, date begun, date finished, a rating of easy, average, or hard, and a scale of 1 (worst) to 5 (best). With portfolios, the reading record has taken on new meaning since students can see the lists from each term together in front of them. By term three Amber had three reading lists in her folder pocket, and the assessment process had become much more concrete in terms of what these records showed about her, in addition to her feelings about herself as a reader.

Loose-leaf notebooks turned out to be my favorite portfolio method. It is easy to flip forward and backward through a student's work, nothing has to be pulled out and shuffled through, and many of the students become better organized by using this format. The only pitfall was the need to be careful and accurate when punching holes in papers. Many students made their own dividers between subjects using construction paper, which they had custom-fitted and decorated with the subject title and sometimes a table of contents within the subject.

Photo albums were also very effective. I found it interesting that Katie, who had spent a lot of time constructing a nonfunctional portfolio the first time around, was the one who came up with the idea of using photo albums during a discussion about what was going well with our portfolios and what we wanted to change. The photo albums were great for demonstrating growth in a student's work. Students just peeled back a plastic sheet, placed a page of work where the photographs usually go, and smoothed the plastic cover back. This worked well for reading lists, spelling tests, learning log entries, and other items that were one page long. For work that was longer, students used the photo album like a loose-leaf notebook and included papers punched with three holes.

These are the five kinds of portfolio cases my students developed as they worked with and reflected on portfolios this year. I think it was essential for them to have a choice about how they developed their portfolios. I did comment on strong points I noticed as students revised their approaches and reminded them of the purpose of the portfolios: to represent their work.

Portfolio Letters

Because I wanted my students to reflect on their portfolios as a whole, I asked them to write a letter to me about them with the understanding that the audience for the letter would ultimately include their parents. We decided that the letters would tell what was in the portfolio, why it was there, and what it showed about them as learners. The drafts of these letters were treated just like other pieces of writing composed during writing/reading workshop: students drafted, shared, and received feedback about what others liked, learned about, and wanted to hear more about. We also asked questions we thought parents might ask. Sharing provided great models. As with other genres, the portfolio letters improved the more experience students had writing them and the more they responded to other writers and were responded to in turn.

Portfolio Planning

I realized that I needed a way to know what students were planning to put in their portfolios and what they had already put in. The first time they created portfolios I had each student write down a specific plan for the contents. The second time around, at the end of term three, I asked if anyone had really looked at their plans once they had written them; the response was no. So we scrapped that idea and came up with a portfolio checklist. As a class we brainstormed subject by subject all the things they had done during the term. The resulting list went on the board and was later transferred to paper and put into a folder so students could look through it to help them reflect on the term's content. Students then made their own rough checklists, which afforded me a quick point of reference as I walked around the room to see where students were in their portfolio work. This is Ryan's writing checklist for term three:

Writing
- Nonfiction example
- Fiction example
- Skills test
- Spelling
- Poetry (3–5 poems)
- Memorized poem

I asked that checklists be kept updated—that areas be checked off as they were completed—and out on desks during workshop time as I circulated and talked with students about their efforts. Once, when a student had checked off fiction on his list, I asked to see what he had included for his sample. It was a short paragraph from a long story that didn't show very much about him as a writer, and he had the opportunity to find a more representative sample before submitting the portfolio at the end of the term.

The checklists help me focus on work in progress, and, based on what I see happening, I can talk to the whole class about the direction their work is taking and guide the direction of the portfolios as they are being made rather than waiting until they are completed. As a colleague described it, I try to lead from behind by asking questions.

Portfolio Conferences

I expect students to complete their portfolios about one week before the term ends. "Complete" means that the contents represent the student as a learner at this point in the school year. Then I have a conference with each student. Beforehand I go through the portfolio and take notes on a record-keeping sheet that has three columns. The left column is where I take my notes. Here I record strengths, changes, improvements, questions, and concerns—any areas I want to address with the student in conference. I take this information to our conference, but I keep my mouth closed and listen to the student first.

I have found it crucial to let students take me through their portfolios at our conferences. I try not to touch the contents. They show me their work. And I try to look at the work as if I have never seen it before and know nothing about it. My most frequent question to students is "What does this show about you?" In the far right column of my record-keeping sheet I record their observations about their work and their responses to my questions. The conversation is focused on the work in front of us. If a student tells me that he or she has improved in an area, I ask if the portfolio shows this.

For example, in our conference, Jim told me that his writing had improved a lot because he was using more details and "showing more than telling." I asked him if the piece he had chosen to represent his writing showed this improvement. He said it did and started reading part of it out loud. After a moment he stopped and said, "You know, this doesn't have much detail. I think that should still be a goal of mine for next term." I asked if it was just because he hadn't chosen his best sample, but he said no, he really needed to improve in this area. In this way, evaluation becomes concrete because we constantly refer to the specific work in front of us. On those occasions when a student felt he or she had improved in an area but the portfolio sample didn't show that growth, we brainstormed ways to revise the sample.

Record Keeping

As I mentioned, my record-keeping sheet has three columns: one for my responses, one for students' responses, and a middle column for goals for next term. This organization represents a coming together of my perceptions and those of my students. If I see an area that needs strengthening yet the student hasn't mentioned it, we discuss it, and it becomes a new goal. Students often set more appropriate and challenging goals than the ones I come up with, as my experience with Ryan illustrates.

As I studied Ryan's portfolio at the end of term three, I noted my concerns about his reading. He had finished only two books during terms one and two and was on his third book for term three. I wrote in the teacher comment column that I was concerned about his effort and reading pace. I wanted him to set a goal for himself of reading more.

During our conference, I asked Ryan what his three reading lists showed about him as a reader. Ryan became very animated as he told me, "I've found tons of good books this year. Like *Hatchet*—it's a great adventure. I'm not a very fast reader, but I understand what I read. They read a lot faster, but I bet they can't tell as much about what they read as I can."

"They," in Ryan's quote, referred to Hal, who sat in the same response group as Ryan and literally read a book a day. Ryan also mentioned that he liked to reread pages and that he is a morning person. Sometimes he reads in bed lying down, but he gets really tired doing that, so one goal of his is going to be to sit up in bed to read. He mentioned that he had already read more books this year than all of last year. He said that sometimes he forgets his books at school and has nothing to read at home. We talked about this and agreed that his main goal for reading would be to remember to take his books home.

Thank goodness I had kept my mouth shut. In focusing on quantity with Ryan, I had missed the point. Until recently, Ryan had a history of difficulty with reading. Then he discovered the novels of Matt Christopher. I had forgotten about where he was as a reader, as my concern over quantity indicated. Listening to Ryan talk about his work gave me the complete picture. I don't know how I attempted an accurate assessment of students' work before we started using portfolios.

I also learned about how students felt about themselves in relation to the subjects under study. Ryan wrote about math in his portfolio letter:

> Two of my favorite things to do this term were % (percentages) and problem solving because I had fun doing them and I feel that I learned a lot, for example 0000000 000 = 70%. I feel good about it. What I've learned about myself is that I thought that I couldn't do fractions as good as I can. Now I feel better about myself. I want to do better at word problems because I feel I can do better at word problems.

Another student, Jeff, wrote about essay tests in social studies. After immersing themselves in the Revolutionary War, the kids had taken a test that included five essay questions the class had generated on themes or concepts about the war that they felt they should know. Jeff had really bombed on the essay section. In his evaluation I learned why. Jeff wrote, "I had a hard time writing the essay questions because I knew more about the Boston Tea Party but I didn't put it in the answer. I thought you just put in what was really, really important."

In our conference, when we talked about Jeff's misconception of essay tests, I learned that he thought of them as outlines. He is now aware that an essay test is a place to demonstrate all of what he knows about a subject. Jeff's goal for social studies became "to show what I know when it comes to essay questions." Again, I was impressed with what I learned about students when I asked them to tell me what their portfolio showed about them. I had assumed that Jeff hadn't applied himself during the test. Out of a poor test score came a valuable, lasting lesson for Jeff and for me, because of the portfolio conference.

Parental Response

When reporting student progress to parents, I write a narrative based on the outcome of the portfolio conference, the student's strengths, and the goals the student plans to work on. Parents' response to the portfolios and the concrete evidence of their children's growth was very positive. Before the portfolios went home I wrote a letter explaining our work. Then, because I wanted to be sure that students had a chance to take their parents through their portfolios as they had me, the class and I talked about asking their parents when would be a good time to sit down and talk. I could imagine my students going home and trying to set up appointments with their parents. (At parent conferences I did hear some funny stories about this.)

In a questionnaire that I included with the letter to parents, I asked what impressed them about their child's portfolio, whether it helped them, what they wanted to know more about, and what questions or suggestions they had for me. Parents were generally impressed with the pride their children showed in themselves and their work as they shared the portfolios. A number of parents felt that it was helpful to see a comprehensive, concrete picture of the specific work we were doing in school. One parent said that the portfolio helped her visualize the report card. Parents' concerns included spelling errors and the kind of specific skills the students were acquiring. They also wanted to see more math.

I shared this parent feedback with my students, and they decided they needed to work harder on editing the portfolio letters. Since in our spelling program students learn to find and correct the words they misspell in their writing, the portfolios provided a lot of practice in finding, circling, and correcting misspellings. I jotted "sp" on a line that contained a misspelled word, and these misspellings were to be entered into the student's own "misspeller's dictionary," on which each writer was tested weekly. This was hard work, and it helped us develop a better peer-editing system. Labeling portfolio work also became very important because there were pieces of writing, such as log entries, that were not meant to be polished pieces.

In April students came up with a great solution to their parents' wish to see more evidence of skill growth: they decided to pick a piece of writing from September and edit it. Afterwards I asked them to jot down their reactions on the back of the edited pieces. Students and parents saw very clearly which skills had improved and which still needed work. As Kylie commented in her portfolio letter, "And I thought I learned all I needed to know about skills in the fourth grade!"

Parents' desire to see more math also told me what they valued. During the next term, I asked the class to increase the amount of work they chose to represent themselves as math students. This was especially important because we were using a lot of manipulatives, a new concept for many of the parents.

Because the portfolios helped enhance communication with parents by offering a clear picture of school, they became a vital link between children's home and school lives.

Final Portfolios

At the end of the year the portfolio took on a broader perspective. I asked students to look back through their earlier work and see what they noticed. Because of the time span involved, this last portfolio of the year grew to be the most valuable one. The students saw striking growth when they looked at what they had done in September and October.

Many students included a science experiment from the fall and another from the late spring in the final portfolios. The write-ups of the fall experiment tended toward superficial observations; in contrast, the spring experiments included materials needed, observations, hypotheses, and conclusions. For example, in summarizing her October plant experiment, Katie wrote: "[My plant] is a lot lighter at the top of the plant and the leaves are practically yellow," while her account of her May steam and bottle experiment, in which a balloon placed over the mouth of an empty bottle expanded when heated and was pulled into the bottle when cooled, included a different kind of thinking: "I think this happened because the steam made the molecules spread farther apart so there wasn't room for something else such as the balloon to come into the bottle because it took up so much space. But when the molecules got cold there was room for the balloon, so it got sucked in and started to blow up [inside the bottle]." These two conclusions set side by side clearly demonstrated an increased involvement with increasingly sophisticated concepts. The fall/spring comparison of pieces of writing and other content subjects was also effective and dramatic.

Goals for Next Year

First and foremost, I am interested in inviting students next year to view portfolios as an ongoing process, something they keep in mind every day as they work and become more aware of examples of exceptional thinking. If their portfolios are in their thoughts throughout the term, they may have less collating to do at the end, which will save class time.

I also plan to invite parents *and* students to come to parent conferences. I think this would further strengthen the link between school and home. I envision students taking us through their portfolios. This year parents loved hearing what their children had told me about the portfolios and comparing it to what they said at home, so why not put it all together?

Recently, during a summer course I taught, I developed portfolios with adult students. They wanted to see how others in the class had used portfolios, so they paired up, swapped, and wrote response letters to their partners. The letters were so valuable that they included them in the portfolios. I also noticed a spreading of ideas and techniques. Using partners worked so well with adults I would like to try this kind of sharing with next year's fifth graders.

I am also considering including photographs of student projects and performances, and I'm looking for ways to incorporate different kinds of portfolios by involving the local business community—graphic artists, photographers, jewelers, and architects—and engaging students in a discussion of the similarities and differences that we see in their portfolios. But the real key, next year and always, is to keep portfolios fluid, changing, and responsive—and to keep the students at the center.

References

Carter, Forrest. 1976. *The Education of Little Tree.* Albuquerque: University of New Mexico Press.

Paulsen, Gary. 1987. *Hatchet.* New York: Viking Penguin.

EVALUATION:
WHAT'S REALLY GOING ON?

LYNN PARSONS
Stratham Memorial School
Stratham, New Hampshire

*W*hen I came to Stratham Memorial School in 1985 as a third-grade teacher, it had been a writing process school for two years. We used a traditional reporting system, with letter grades based on percentages. There was no section on our report card for writing, so it was through the language arts section that we evaluated student writing. Since most of us felt uncomfortable evaluating writing process instruction, our grades reflected the quality of students' effort rather than their finished products. It wasn't great, but we could live with it.

During the next school year the staff began to explore a reading process approach as well. By spring, all of Stratham's classroom teachers had abandoned basals and were immersed —happily—in reading with trade books. Gone were the worksheets, workbooks, and skills in isolation. Students were reading, really reading, and developing as responsible, mature readers in ways we had not anticipated. Needless to say, we were excited about the new direction our reading instruction was taking.

But, inevitably, report card time rolled around, and we were faced with a new dilemma—how to grade students' reading progress. As distasteful and irrelevant to real reading as they now seemed, the workbooks, worksheets, basal questions, and basal tests had provided us with information that could be fashioned into a letter grade. Again, we did the best we could. And again, our grades reflected effort, not achievement.

Even before the switch from basals we had felt uncomfortable using letter grades to evaluate reading. What did a *C* mean? Did the student have trouble with the workbook pages? Difficulty with testing? Maybe he or she didn't answer the basal questions completely or couldn't keep up with the rest of the reading group.

The letter grade was an inaccurate reporting tool even when used with the traditional basal reading system. Now, since we no longer did workbooks, worksheets, and basal tests, and there were no longer reading groups to "keep up" with, our reporting system in no way reflected what we were asking students to do as readers every day in our classrooms.

What was going on in our reading classes? And how could we accurately report this information to parents? These were the questions we asked ourselves as the school year drew to a close. It seemed apparent that we needed to devise a new tool to evaluate students as readers and to take a hard look at our evaluation of writing process.

Our principal had been understanding and asked us to do the best we could with the old reporting system. But even he realized that the time had come to revise the report card. With his full support we formed a committee of six classroom teachers, ranging from first through fifth grade, to work on constructing a new reporting model.

One of our committee members was Janis Bailey, a newly hired third-grade teacher who had been a reading specialist in Maine. She brought with her a literacy evaluation system that she and her former colleagues had developed (Bailey et al. 1988). Although the tool we finally devised is quite different, we were definitely guided by the tone and intent of the other system. It helped to channel our thinking in new ways, away from traditional checklists of skills and toward specific student behaviors.

At our first meeting, as we began to talk about the shape our new reporting system might take, again and again we found ourselves making strong connections between reading and writing, just as the students in our classrooms were doing. A discussion about students making sense of what they read led to the realization that they also make sense of what they write. We talked of trying different genres in reading as well as writing, and of sharing our reading and writing. The correlations went on and on. Would it perhaps be possible to design a report card that would directly relate reading and writing? We began to break reading and writing into some basic complementary components.

As we worked, we constantly asked ourselves, what is it we

ask students to do when they read and write? We started at the beginning, with the initiation of their own reading and writing. We felt it was important in a process classroom, where much responsibility for decision making is placed on students' shoulders, that they be accountable for being prepared to work and for getting down to work in both reading and writing. And if students were expected to take responsibility for their own learning, they needed to make decisions about what they would read and write.

We also spent a great deal of time discussing comprehension. It was important that students be able to use a variety of approaches to make meaning out of what they read. They also needed to develop their ability to produce meaningful writing. We did not want this report card to become another checklist of skills, so we decided to keep the evaluation of comprehension broad. What was important to us was that students comprehended, not whether they could specifically sequence, predict, or use context clues in isolation.

Since another important area for us was the sharing of reading and writing through conferences and journals, we decided to include sharing as part of our evaluation system. And because we expected our students to become more responsible for their own learning, we felt it important that they request meaningful help when they needed it. This, too, was added to our list. As we worked, we were excited to see how easily we were able to correlate reading and writing. Within just a few days we were able to come up with a format we liked, with only one concession to parental concerns. We included a "reads materials developed for children at his/her grade level" category. That was as far as we were willing to go in identifying a child's grade level reading ability; fortunately, it seemed to provide parents with sufficient information.

After we had established the format we began work on an evaluation key (see Figure 1). This proved to be more difficult than devising the report card. Should we use numbers? Letters? Checks, pluses, minuses? And what should we do to avoid drawing parallels to traditional grading systems? We tried to word everything positively, with an emphasis on the degree of progress a child was making. The key we eventually settled on has since undergone several changes and, as I write this, is going through yet another revision. We have found it difficult to design a key that says the same thing to everyone who sees it—students, teachers, administrators, and parents. Surprisingly, even among our

Figure 1

Dear Parents,

Stratham Memorial School has recently adopted a process approach to reading that complements our writing program. As a community of learners, we have revised our evaluation instrument for reporting children's progress in reading and writing to reflect what we know about how children learn.

This progress report will explain our observation of your child's development as a reader and writer in relation to the characteristics we have identified in these areas.

In order for you to fully understand this evaluation instrument, the following definitions may be helpful:

- INITIATES: Organizes time and materials, assumes responsibility to begin.
- COMPREHENSION STRATEGIES: Uses background experience and context clues, predicts, confirms, and revises ideas.
- PRINT CUES: Uses phonics, word attack skills, rules of grammar.
- READING JOURNAL:
  Primary Level: Uses pictures and written responses.
  Intermediate Level: Uses written response.
- REVISES IDEAS: Adds, deletes, expands, re-arranges, or clarifies.
- EDITS: Attends to spelling, punctuation, capitalization, and grammar.

OBSERVATIONS ABOUT THE STUDENT AS A LEARNER
PROCESS APPROACH TO READING AND WRITING

READING

QUARTER:	1	2	3	4
INITIATES OWN READING				
CHOOSES READING MATERIALS				
ACTIVELY PARTICIPATES IN READING DISCUSSION GROUPS				
SHARES OWN READING				
USES APPROPRIATE PRINT CUES TO DEVELOP MEANING (PHONICS, PUNCTUATION, PARAGRAPHING, ETC.)				
REQUESTS MEANINGFUL HELP IN READING AS NEEDED				
USES APPROPRIATE COMPREHENSION STRATEGIES TO GAIN MEANING				
WRITES EFFECTIVE JOURNAL RESPONSES TO LITERATURE				
READS MATERIALS DEVELOPED FOR CHILDREN AT HIS/HER GRADE LEVEL				
EXHIBITS EFFORT				

WRITING

QUARTER:	1	2	3	4
INITIATES OWN WRITING				
CHOOSES WRITING TOPICS				
ACTIVELY PARTICIPATES IN WRITING CONFERENCES				
SHARES OWN WRITING				
USES APPROPRIATE PRINT CUES TO DEVELOP MEANING (PHONICS, PUNCTUATION, PARAGRAPHING, ETC.)				
REQUESTS MEANINGFUL HELP IN WRITING AS NEEDED				
REVISES IDEAS WHEN APPROPRIATE				
PRODUCES MEANINGFUL WRITING				
EDITS WHEN APPROPRIATE (MECHANICS)				
EXHIBITS EFFORT				

KEY TO PROGRESS:

1 =	EXCELLENT PROGRESS
2 =	STEADY PROGRESS
3 =	ACCEPTABLE PROGRESS
4 =	NOT PROGRESSING AS EXPECTED
X =	NOT EVALUATED AT THIS TIME

COMMENTS:

own staff we have found drastically different interpretations and uses of the key. We continue to try to iron this out. And the school never prints so many copies of the report card that we cannot afford to change our minds about the current system and tinker with format and language.

I am happy, and a bit surprised, to report that our reading/writing report card has stayed almost exactly the same as we first designed it. It continues to be a system we are comfortable using because it is our own and because it reflects what we know about and value in reading and writing. Figure 1 shows the latest version and key, as well as the brief letter we sent to parents. I include it here not as a model report card but as a demonstration of how teachers who share a theory of literacy and a commitment to process approaches can help parents understand what the school values about literacy and what individual children can do as readers and writers.

Reference

Bailey, Janis, et al. 1988. "Problem-Solving Our Way to Alternative Evaluation Procedures." *Language Arts* 65 (4):364–73.

A Guest Essay
THE MIDDLE CLASS
AND THE PROBLEM
OF PLEASURE

THOMAS NEWKIRK
University of New Hampshire

*I*t is open season on the young. Hardly a week goes by without some report on their failings—in math, geography, writing, civics, or history. They can't find Canada. They don't know who the Head of the Joint Chiefs of Staff is (but we now know that Ronald Reagan didn't either). Virtually every special interest group seems to be testing students, sending out press releases on their weaknesses, and using the results to ask for more federal money—or for a uniform curriculum that they would write.

A fairly typical report on the failings of the young appeared in a recent *Boston Globe* under the headline "America's Young Have Tuned Out on Politics." It opens ominously:

> A young American coming of age in the 1990's has mastered computer games but cannot name his congressman. He is, by and large, a political illiterate, and this is generating anxiety about the future vitality of democracy in the United States.

And within two sentences it becomes apocalyptic:

> Students of government and politics worry that the United States is breeding a generation of self-centered know-nothings whose disengagement threatens the founding fathers' great experiment in its third century.

These willfully ignorant young people have forgotten that "freedom carries a price tag," and unless they get their act together "government may soon become the exclusive domain of extremists and special interest groups."

The contempt for the young—for our own children—in this

63

report can only make sense as a kind of projection, as indirect discourse that says more about what we adults think of (and fear about) ourselves than what we deplore in our children. As any parent knows, the "faults" in our children that irritate us the most are those that mirror our own. We see our worst selves reflected back at us. *The Boston Globe* can criticize the young for being self-centered, but it is, after all, the adult culture (less than half of which bothers to vote) that has supported policies that have piled up federal debt for the young to pay. Which is the pot and which the kettle?

It is this kind of projection that makes my topic, evaluation, so slippery. It would be far easier to treat evaluation as a technical problem that can be "solved." If we could look at schools in isolation from the adult culture, if we could assume that we had a totally free hand in evaluation, the problem would not be as complex as it is. We could discuss portfolio assessments and the variety of work that would go into portfolios. We could get together in groups to look at samples and drafts of student writing and agree on broad goals for writing. In the area of reading we could talk of varieties of running records and informal assessments. None of this is easy. But if that were all we had to do—if this were primarily a technical problem—the question of evaluation would not tie us in knots the way it does.

Or we could admit that it is a political problem but one in which there are clearly defined good guys and bad guys. The good guys (Graves, Harste, Hansen, Atwell, the Goodmans, Shannon—you can add others) are for kids. The bad guys (the testmakers, basal companies, cultural literacists, parents who want more "basics") are—if the truth were to be told—against kids. We trust kids; they don't. We could turn the question of evaluation into a morality play—process versus product, liberation versus oppression, good versus bad. But as much as I would like to be on the side of the angels, I'm not comfortable believing that people who disagree with me are against children. They're for them in a different way.

I want to argue that the issue of evaluation is fundamentally related to the fears, hopes, self-doubts, and frequently contradictory expectations projected onto schools by a powerful, professional middle class. And to understand the often ambivalent attitude of these parents toward innovations like "the writing process" or "whole language," we must attend carefully to what Barbara Ehrenreich (1989) has called "the inner life of the middle class."

". . . . . but . . . . ."

A few weeks ago I was asked to be on a panel at a parent meeting in an elementary school that has had a long association with the University of New Hampshire, one that won a national award for excellence and was visited by William Bennett, then Secretary of Education, who taught a lesson on the Constitution. Teachers at the school have been active in professional organizations; they work closely with each other. The school is mentioned in real estate advertisements. I thought that if any school should have the support of the community, this one should. But—the principal told me that parents were concerned and that I should be prepared.

The meeting began at 7:00. There was a forty-minute panel presentation, and then it was time for questions. A half hour, an hour, an hour and a half. The questioning was not hostile or fundamentally critical. Most of the questions took the same form:

- I'm glad my child is able to use invented spelling, but I'm concerned he won't be able to spell correctly.
- My child is enjoying reading and I'm grateful for that, but I wonder if she's getting the necessary skills.
- I like the freedom my child has, but is he being challenged?
- I like the philosophy of the program, but what happens when they go to the junior high school?
- I like the fact that students aren't grouped by ability, but will my child be held back?

Always the "but." The tension in the voices of the parents was palpable. Their uneasiness was palpable. Their concern for their children was palpable. The principal finally called the meeting at 9:30. Almost no one had left.

As the principal said to me after the meeting, there were a lot of new parents and they needed to be informed—that information was the real issue. I'm not so sure. I think we had seen the middle class in action. The "but" in the middle of these sentences reflected a central conflict in the goals they have for their children. And this internal conflict makes evaluation difficult.

Who makes up this middle class? Go to a T-ball game and these parents, during the interminable innings, will be sharing information on teachers like scouts talking about young pitchers. Check out the parent organizations and they will be prominent. On parent nights both father and mother often attend. Some other indicators:

- This is the class that, when choosing a house to buy, asks first about the schools.
- This is the class that tries to micro-manage their child's progress through school. Parents attend carefully to reports about teachers and feel that each year there should be a match. A "bad year," they feel, will put their child at a serious competitive disadvantage.
- This is the class that sees itself as the social and professional equal of teachers, administrators, and school board members. They are willing to question procedures and to be strong advocates for their children.
- This is the class that can consider the option of private schooling, although such schooling would mean a great financial sacrifice. When they hear rumors of drugs in the local public high school, they automatically think of the local Catholic high school.

We know these people. To some degree we are these people. But I want to look beyond these more obvious identifiers to what Ehrenreich has called their "inner lives" and the reasons for their anxiety about public schooling.

We can start with the idea of entitlement. What do middle-class, professional parents pass on to their children? Historically parents pass on wealth or land or a trade or a position in a factory or company. But, ironically, middle-class professionals have set up and supported systems of credentials—hurdles—that their own children must surmount. Take my case. I have worked over the past few years to set up doctoral programs in both the Education and English Departments. And I am, as a professional, happy that we can offer degrees in composition and literacy education. But my daughter Sarah, who some day may want to teach writing in college, will have to earn these degrees. I've created a hurdle she must jump.

What the middle class seeks to offer children is a sense of discipline, of directedness, of purposefulness that will help them succeed at the long apprenticeships necessary for them to join the professional middle class—four years of college to be followed by graduate school or law school. We want to give them an inner compass that will keep them on target even though they must postpone earning any real income until their late twenties. (I was thirty before I earned ten thousand dollars a year.) Ehrenreich writes:

Thus the barriers that the middle class erected to protect itself made it painfully difficult to reproduce itself. It is one thing to have children, and another thing to have children who will be disciplined enough to devote the first twenty or thirty years of their lives to scaling the educational obstacles to a middle-class career. Nor is there any obvious, reliable way the older generation can help. All parents can do is attempt, through psychological pressure, to predispose each child to retrace the long journey they themselves took. (83)

This concern explains, I believe, the near epidemic of lessons that children take after school—gymnastics, soccer, musical instruments, dance. I don't think it is too cynical to argue that one thing parents are buying is *discipline*. The child who will practice the violin every night (instead of watching "The Simpsons" or "The Cosby Show") is developing discipline, a capacity to delay gratification. Whatever the child's future musical career, that attitude, the rich residue of those lessons, will remain.

This leads to a second paradox—the problem of affluence. Middle-class professionals can afford to provide the extras for their children—the trip to Disneyworld, the Nintendo games, regular attendance at movies, money for trips to the mall, visits to Toys R Us—and, of course, cable TV, where rock videos and cartoons are available at almost any time of the day. Affluence allows us to provide these gratifications and we do, although with nagging misgivings.

For the dilemma is obvious. This affluence can undermine the very qualities our children will eventually need to become middle-class professionals. *The lurking fear in the hearts of middle-class parents is that they—that we—are spoiling our children.* Our children will grow soft, and we will be the cause. The immediate gratifications of the consumer, media culture—things we provide them—will weaken, perhaps fatally, their capacity for delayed gratification. The exposed nerve of the middle class is this fear of permissiveness. As a result, the middle class looks for support to community lesson-givers, and to the major community lesson-giver, the schools.

Ehrenreich's book explains for me the curious tolerance the middle class has for school activities that seem dull and repetitive. I am not saying they all support mechanical approaches to reading and writing, but clearly there has been no revolt. We don't see middle-class parents marching because something as pleasurable as reading has been turned into such joyless work in so many schools. In fact, the middle class has a genius for turning pleasure into work—or at least turning pleasure into something strenuous and competitive.

One incident stands out in my mind. It was a beautiful summer day and I was picking my daughter up at the Y (where, true to my argument, she was taking a gymnastics lesson). The Y is new and is far different from the Y that I went to as a kid. There, the central space was the gym where we "played" basketball or kickball or volleyball. The central place in this new Y was an exercise room where adults could "work" out. I looked in the room, and there was someone walking a treadmill. He was sweating and serious and I'm sure he was getting all kind of readouts on how fast and how far he was walking, although to my eyes he wasn't getting anywhere. Even the word "treadmill" is synonymous with drudgery and pointlessness. But here he was, on this beautiful Saturday, just a few miles from the beachwalk in Rye, walking a treadmill.

We do the same thing to language learning that this man did to walking—turn pleasure into work. Work activities virtually replace the pleasurable act of reading in schools. Students sit at work areas filling in worksheets pulled from workbooks—all the while developing good work habits. The reading they do should be on their "instructional level"; that is, they should have trouble with at least four percent of the words. Otherwise they won't be working hard enough. I know one writing/reading process teacher who had trouble with parents because her students said they didn't "work" in her class—they just read books they liked, wrote, drew, and discussed. Now she is careful to call all of these activities "work."

This attitude—that schoolwork should encourage a capacity for delayed gratification—creates real problems when it comes to teaching literature. Reading literature is deeply pleasurable. It gives us enjoyment. It makes us laugh. It moves us. Sometimes university English departments don't want to admit that. How can you justify the largest department on the campus on the basis that it promotes pleasure-seeking? It sounds immoral.

So we turn pleasure into work. At the elementary level we introduce workbooks and worksheets. At the high school and college level, there is an obsessional push to teach certain classic texts. Do not misunderstand me: I love many of these texts. My interest here is in the motives of those who push for the classics. The concern for the classics is, I feel, a coded argument for discipline, for delayed gratification. To read, perhaps prematurely (maybe especially prematurely), a book like *Moby-Dick* or *The Iliad* requires a capacity to sustain attention through a lot of material the younger reader will not understand. It requires the student to believe the experience valuable, even when he or she might find the reading dull. This persistence, of course, builds character and self-discipline. Whatever the young reader remembers from these books, self-discipline will be the true, valuable residue of the experience. Thus the appeal, I believe, of the classics. Books with a more ready appeal—*The Chocolate War* or *Catcher in the Rye*—are suspect because of the immediate pleasure they might provide.

If I am right that a fear of permissiveness is the exposed nerve of the middle class, then we can understand the ambivalence that many in this class feel about reading and writing process instruction as they are commonly argued for. Typically the notion of choice figures large in descriptions of what we do. Students should choose books and writing topics, and the teacher's job is often described by some euphemism like *facilitator*. To actually teach would be too great an intrusion into the sanctity of the student's decision making. We are trapped by organic metaphors that suggest that the child's "unfolding" will be hindered if the teacher has objectives for that unfolding. We use misleading metaphors of property—"ownership"—that invariably imply that the teacher is an outsider in the learning process.

These arguments can sound dangerously permissive, soft, and indulgent to some parents. If fear of spoiling is a central fear, then arguments for choice may not be reassuring. Schools can be seen as extensions of a multiple-gratifying consumer culture, where the child can choose from dozens of cable channels. If enjoyment becomes a key criteria in the selection of reading books and writing topics, how will children develop the capacity to persevere in tasks that, at least initially, are not enticing?

But—always the but—these parents also appreciate the interest their children show, their enthusiasm for reading and writing. And when pressed, they will say that they themselves did not particularly enjoy their own schooling. Any English teacher faces the following situation. Someone asks you what you do and you say, a little evasively, that you teach. "Oh, what do you teach?" "English." The person usually takes a couple of steps back, mumbles something like, "That was my worst subject," and tries to find the easiest way to get out of the conversation. They know, at some level, that the "good old days" were dull and, particularly in the area of writing, did not instill in them a sense of self-confidence or feeling of adequacy.

Reclaiming the "Standards" Argument

I am suggesting that we may be using the wrong tactics in arguing for a more open approach to writing and reading. If we stress child-centeredness and the lack of teacher direction, the almost divine right of the child to choose from a wide array of options the teacher helps place before him or her, then we may appear more permissive than we are. We are often trapped into a rhetoric of freedom that makes it difficult to acknowledge our own influence in the process classroom. By stressing process over product (as if they can be separated), we fail to demonstrate that we expect a high quality of writing from students—and usually get it. We need to learn how to say the word *excellence* without stuttering.

For too long the technocrats and the educational right wing have monopolized the standards argument. They are tough-minded and rigorous. We are soft, indulgent, catering to the whims of students. On the issue of standardized tests, for example, we always find ourselves in a no-win situation—either we support them or we appear to be hiding our misdeeds. And as long as we stress the child-centered rationale for our teaching, we allow the technocrats and the right to use the standards argument against us. I think it's time we reclaimed that argument.

To begin, we can show parents what standardized tests ask of children and compare that to the kind of work students do in classrooms. For the past year I have been recording discussions that first graders hold in reading groups; so far I've transcribed six hundred pages. Next week these students take their achievement tests. The disparity between what they do in discussion groups and "comprehension" as it is defined in these tests is shocking. In the tests, they are to look at a picture and pick a word that doesn't fit the picture. The danger, as I see it, is that the student think creatively—in which case more than one word might fit. Pity the student that thinks.

We can also emphasize high expectations in the amount of reading and writing we ask of students. The folders of drafts, the logs of books read, are powerful evidence that children are getting more practice than they would in typical classes. Several years ago, I visited a school where some of our writing program teachers were teaching. It was one of the most conservative districts in our very conservative state. I asked the principal if he had any difficulty explaining the program to parents. "No, not at all," he said. "I say we're going back to basics, and what could be more basic than having children read and write?"

We need to show that we have high standards for those areas that are called "skills"—that spelling, for example, matters—and that we have ways of monitoring student progress and working with them.

Finally, we can demonstrate that we expect self-discipline on the part of the student, a kind of discipline that is impossible when students are led by the nose along the treadmill of workbook activities. Discipline—true discipline—can only come when the student has some choice in the path he or she takes. Without the possibility of choice we aren't asking that students be disciplined, only that they be obedient. If we can show a parent papers that are the result of a sustained and thoughtful process, we are offering evidence of true discipline.

But—always the but. We come back to the troublesome notion of pleasure. Discipline, self-direction, the work ethic, are, after all, rather dour virtues. And without passion, a love of language and of books, they will not take us far. The great contribution of the writing process movement, and ultimately its strongest appeal, does not concern giving freedom to students or asking discipline of them. It concerns pleasure, what Ehrenreich calls the "hedonism of work." More about joy than grit. More about love than duty. Annie Dillard (1987) explains it best in her essay, "To Fashion a Text":

> There's a common notion that self-discipline is a freakish peculiarity among writers—that writers differ from other people by possessing enormous and equal portions of talent and willpower. They grit their powerful teeth and go into their little rooms. I think that is a bad idea of what impels the writer. What impels the writer is a deep love for and respect for language, for literary forms, for books. . . .
>
> Writing a book is like rearing children—willpower has very little to do with it. If you have a little baby crying in the middle of the night, and if you depend only on willpower to get you out of bed to feed the baby, that baby will starve. You do it out of love. Willpower is a weak idea; love is strong. You don't have to scourge yourself with a cat-o'-nine-tails to go to the baby. You go to the baby out of love for that particular baby. That's the same way you go to your desk. There's nothing freakish about it. Caring passionately about something isn't against nature, and it isn't against human nature. It's what we're here to do. (75–76)

For me, the "hedonism of work" illustrated so beautifully in Dillard's description is the capacity to lose yourself in a job, to be in the midst of a project and not be able to estimate the time within an hour, to let go of it reluctantly at the end of a day. Work and pleasure and play seem, for a time, to be merged, indistinguishable. The successful people I know can enter this zone—not always and not for as long as they would like, but they know the way.

Some students are also finding their way there, in classrooms where they can immerse themselves in reading and writing, where they are not listening passively or filling in blanks. And, even if we state the problem in the most pragmatic, business-oriented way, as an economic competition with the Germans and Japanese, they are the ones that will make a difference—because they know how work is done.

References

Black, Chris. 1990. "America's Youth Have Tuned Out on Politics." *Boston Globe*, 13 May, A17.

Dillard, Annie. 1987. "To Fashion a Text." In *Inventing the Truth: The Art and Craft of Memoir*, ed. William Zinsser. Boston: Houghton Mifflin.

Ehrenreich, Barbara. 1989. *Fear of Falling: The Inner Life of the Middle Class*. New York: Pantheon.

SETTING THE STAGE

MIMI DeROSE
Summit Elementary School
Aurora, Colorado

*T*wo and a half years ago a new elementary school was scheduled to open in our district. I remember waiting anxiously to hear who the new principal would be. Before long, news started to spread from school to school. The word was out that the new building, which didn't even have a name yet, was going to be "one of those whole language schools." There was a variety of opinions among teachers within the district about the benefits of whole language, so I knew that those who were hired to teach at the new school would have their work cut out for them.

Openings for positions on the planning team for the new school were posted in February. Those who applied needed a minimum of five years' teaching experience within the district; they also had to be skilled in whole language techniques. Because I supported the philosophy under which the school was to operate and felt that this would be an opportunity for me to grow, personally and professionally, I decided to apply for the grades 5–6 position. After an interview with the principal, I was hired in March.

Initially, four other teachers, the principal, and I formed Summit Elementary School's planning team. Each of the various grade levels was represented, as well as the media center. The planning team's job was to work on the school's philosophy, budget, grade configuration, the hiring of other staff members, and, of course, public relations. Each of the other team members had more experience with whole language strategies in the classroom than I did; however, we all shared a commitment to approaches, to materials, and to a philosophy that we felt would

73

most benefit our students. At the same time, we made a deliberate effort to hire men and women who were not only competent and committed but who would also add some diversity and bring unique strengths to the staff. Each of the twenty teachers hired had a specific talent or area of expertise, including music, art, science, computers, and early childhood education.

During the months before the school opened, many parents expressed concern about how we were going to teach and what materials we were going to use. I think one of the biggest lessons I have learned is the importance of being proactive. By that I don't mean that we need simply to be willing to answer the questions that come from the community; we need to raise the questions ourselves. Several years ago a parent said to me, "You know, when information comes out of a school in a way that sounds as if you're defending something, it automatically makes people start to feel anxious about what's going on." We knew we needed community support before school began. With only a few months in which to get the school up and running, time was valuable. If all of our efforts were spent correcting misinformation or answering the same questions over and over again, we would not have adequate time to organize the staff and make decisions about the school's day-to-day operations.

The members of the planning team agreed that it was important to be honest and articulate when we spoke with our students' parents. We also decided to steer clear of jargon, which not only fails to impress people but may even alienate and anger them. We made a conscious effort to avoid phrases like "whole language," since they really didn't tell anyone anything specific about what we and their children would be doing.

In April we held a community meeting in the school cafeteria. Each team member was responsible for talking to the parents of children who would be enrolled at his or her grade level. Afterward, parents made a number of positive comments about the meeting. They enjoyed the opportunity to talk to teachers who were well versed in a process approach to education, and they appreciated the practical examples that we shared. One teacher had shown a sequence of overhead transparencies that demonstrated the progress of a story written by one of her primary students. By explaining the steps the child went through to arrive at a finished piece, the teacher helped parents understand the rationale behind our writing process approach. And because we used examples of student work instead of talking in general about "the writing process," parents had a real context for asking questions about invented spelling and mechanics.

Another teacher used metaphor to explain the logic behind Summit's philosophy. She drew a picture of an elephant and shared a story about three blind men who were trying to figure out what kind of animal it was. The first man felt the trunk and could describe its characteristics. The second felt an ear and could talk about its features. But the third blind man felt the whole animal and could tell the others exactly what the creature was like. At Summit, our students would learn in the context of whole activities and experiences, not piecemeal.

Parents commented, "This makes sense" or "I had really never thought about it that way" at the end of our presentations. But what was most striking to me was the sense that parents were less concerned about how their children were taught than about the character of the people who would teach them.

We also held a series of smaller neighborhood meetings over the course of a month during the summer that were attended by the principal, a staff member, and neighborhood parents. These meetings took place in homes, and the atmosphere was relaxed and casual. Parents who would not normally speak up in a formal meeting felt comfortable asking questions in a setting removed from the school. Unlike those at the community meeting, the questions at the neighborhood sessions were not usually related to academic aspects of the school. More often parents asked questions that expressed concern for their children's well-being: "What arrangements have been made to make sure our children are safe walking home from school?" "What arrangements will be made for our daughter, who is assigned to a learning disabilities program?" "What can we expect the school to do if there are problems with middle-school students before or after school?"

I learned that just as teachers like to be included in making decisions about their school, so do parents. It can't happen all the time because it simply is not practical. Problems involving the school environment—traffic patterns, schedules, lunch room procedures—demand immediate attention and solutions. There are also aspects of teaching, such as classroom management, that depend upon the temperament and philosophy of the individual teacher and require some flexibility. But there are certainly many opportunities for parents to have a voice in the decisions that have to be made if a school is going to work for its students.

Our Parent Teacher Organization was a tremendous asset to the school during the first year. As soon as school began, the P.T.O. president attended every weekly staff meeting and communicated the decisions we made to the P.T.O. officers and subcommittees. In addition, she met with the principal at least once a week in order to share concerns and seek answers to parents' questions. This made it much less likely that information about the school would become distorted in the larger community. For example, many schools in our area honor parent requests for children to be placed in specific teachers' classrooms. It is our school's policy that unless a parent has already had an unsatisfactory experience with a teacher or a teacher has had an unsatisfactory experience with a parent, requests for classroom placement are not accepted. We discussed this policy at a staff meeting attended by the P.T.O. president; she, in turn, shared the information at a P.T.O. meeting. As a result, most parents know what to expect at the beginning of each year, and class placement is not an issue. In addition to helping us figure out solutions to smaller, "housekeeping" issues, the P.T.O. president has solicited information about how teachers can best use the talents of volunteers, asked for our opinions about fund-raising activities and dates, and helped us list priorities for school expenditures.

Our school also formed a parent advisory committee. Its membership is composed of the P.T.O. president, a parent who does not have children in the school, a P.T.O.-appointed district accountability representative, three staff members who teach different grade levels, and the principal. There is also representation by gender and ethnic background. This committee's agenda was to establish goals for the school and share information about ways to meet our students' needs. When it was necessary, we brought in other professionals from within our district to add their perspective on specific topics. At one meeting, our director of testing and evaluation explained the need for developing alternative assessments. At another session we heard from resource teachers who gave presentations and answered questions about how they work with students placed in such special programs as gifted and talented, mental health counseling, and the learning lab. The committee also set goals to be implemented during the following year; currently these include ways to improve our science program, develop the writing process across the curriculum, and create a positive school climate by continuing to build relationships among students, parents, and staff.

Parent-teacher conference time was also a critical issue in our minds as we reached out to our community. The majority of these conferences are scheduled during two days in October and March when children do not attend school; the rest are held before and after school during these two weeks. At conference time, each grade level team set up chairs around a decorated table offering refreshments and displaying a variety of student projects, including published stories, books, and math and science activities. Parents who had a convenient opportunity to view their children's accomplishments felt more comfortable with what we were doing. Afterward, parents wrote notes to our principal that expressed positive feelings about the school's program and environment.

In our district, each elementary school develops its own forms for reporting student progress. Perhaps the most exciting example of parent involvement at Summit occurred during the development of our reporting system. We knew we needed an evaluation format that would address our needs as teachers of reading and writing, but we also knew that it was important to develop a format parents could easily understand and support. Over a series of meetings a committee of three parents, four teachers, and the principal examined a variety of report cards from different schools and discussed the characteristics of each. As one teacher on the committee put it, "We decided we wanted to come up with something that would give us a picture of each child rather than a lot of detailed information about splinter skills." The result was Summit's learning profile: a detailed assessment of each student's progress that combines a narrative section for each area of social and academic development with a checklist for skills, attitudes, and behaviors. I don't want to imply that one hundred percent of the community believes this is the best reporting format they've ever seen, but the number of dissatisfied parents is no greater than the number who prefer letter grades, percentages, or some other method of reporting.

Summit Elementary has also involved parents in writing grant proposals, because parents' input has helped give us a different perspective on the needs of the school. Last spring four parents and four teachers successfully applied for a Chapter 2 grant that will enable us to help at-risk students and will also provide training in parenting skills. In the process of writing the proposal parents helped us to be more clear and less threatening in our choice of language. It wasn't uncommon to hear them say, "I don't think most people understand that kind of language" or

"Parents really like it when they get program invitations that are written by their own children because it personalizes it." Their partnership with the staff helped to increase the support we received from other parents. Because they had firsthand information, they could disseminate news about programs, materials, and in-service training throughout the community.

Finally, in order to experience what it is like to be a learner, each staff member made a commitment to take on new learning experience. Our district has a policy that requires teachers to complete professional growth activities over a certain period of time. Often teachers fulfill these requirements by taking in-service courses or classes at local universities. The first year that Summit was open, each staff member made a commitment to learn something completely new; then we had a year to plan and implement the activities. I decided to attempt to master roller-skates. Some teachers took on new challenges individually, while others formed small groups and learned together. As often as possible we used other staff members as resources. A grade 3–4 teacher taught guitar lessons, and one of our instrumental music teachers included the principal in his beginning violin class. In December the principal participated in a school recital, and by June many faculty members were budding guitar players, tennis players, and acupressure therapists. It was a great opportunity to get to know each other beyond the school setting, and it also gave us tremendous insights into what we expected from our students every day. We understood what it meant to put ourselves on the line in front of our peers. We lived with disappointment when we didn't meet the expectations we had established for ourselves, and we enjoyed feelings of success when we reached our goals.

As a new school adopting an innovative philosophy, Summit Elementary developed approaches to public relations that suited our situation. Established schools, in which teachers already trust and respect each other, may actually have an advantage in cultivating a positive relationship with their communities. They can more easily identify specific goals and develop plans to reach them, and they can also predict parent concerns: What are we doing that parents need to know more about? What questions will they have? What will our responses be? Can we support what we believe with practical examples? What is the best way to make this information available? Established schools can also decide how slowly or quickly to make changes based on their level of staff involvement and community support.

Whether teaching in a brand new or a long-established school, educators who share a genuine concern for everyone associated with the school see the importance of bringing the community along and are willing to go the extra mile. This means that they make additional contacts with parents, serve on parent organization committees, and help out with fund-raisers. It means that principals redefine their roles as administrators by encouraging parent involvement and establishing the groundwork for communications. In some cases, this may require a reevaluation of the balance of power within the school itself.

All of our efforts have produced tremendous rewards. Parents volunteer their help by publishing children's writing, working with small groups, and assisting with special programs. They share their firsthand knowledge of the school's activities within their own homes and neighborhoods and let teachers know how much they appreciate all that is done for their children. But it is in students' attitudes that the impact of a healthy relationship with the community is greatest. Our students reflect their parents' enthusiastic feelings about school and learning.

The process of building a bond between a school and its community is never ending, because the need to maintain positive community relations is vital to the success of any school. But a school that uses innovative approaches has a particular responsibility to work in partnership with parents. Ultimately, it is their values and priorities that determine the school's direction. Parents need to know that the school will provide many opportunities for them to ask questions and voice their concerns, and teachers need to understand that it is our responsibility to put ourselves in a parent's place: innovative models look different from what parents remember of their own schoolwork, and parents often have a different perspective on their children's needs than teachers do. There are still community members who have doubts about the methods we are using at Summit, but I believe that the number of concerns is small because of the attention the community receives from the school and the many roles that parents play in the life of the school. I also believe it is healthy for teachers to constantly evaluate our attitudes and approaches, and the community can help us do this.

Two years ago when I applied to teach at Summit, I was looking for opportunities for personal and professional growth. I discovered that they are one and the same. Maintaining strong relationships with my students' parents is an ongoing process that is as necessary as editing student writing, planning field trips, and finding new literature to share. I have learned much from my principal, my colleagues, and my students' parents because of their willingness to share ideas, troubleshoot problems, and celebrate each other's accomplishments.

The Teacher Interview
TOBY KAHN CURRY
AND DEBRA GOODMAN

AN INTERVIEW BY YETTA GOODMAN
WITH COMMENTARY BY KEN GOODMAN

*T*oby Kahn Curry and Debra Goodman teach at the Dewey Center for Urban Education, a public, whole language magnet school, which they proposed and initiated in inner-city Detroit. As of this writing the school has finished its first rocky year and has a waiting list.

More than most teachers, Toby and Debi have experienced how very political education is, particularly urban education. A conversation between Toby, Debi, and Yetta has been distilled by Ken to focus on how the two teachers learned to work through and around the politics.

Theory and Practice

Toby and Debi knew that whole language teachers are under a lot of pressure and get little administrative support for the risks they take and the innovations they try. Teachers are treated as technicians who need to be told what to do and who aren't interested in understanding why they should do things differently.

YETTA: This is a very important issue for me. My own colleagues at the university level keep saying things like, "Teachers only want to know what to do on Monday, they don't care about theory."

DEBI: I think it's a cycle. A group of teachers from a district that decided to pilot whole language comes to our support group meetings. They know little about whole language, and nobody in their system is capable of consulting with them. And they're supposed to be piloting whole language for the district. It's a pressure-cooker situation. So for many teachers I think the immediate question is "How am I going to get through the next week?"

A few years ago I heard some Canadian teachers talk about their first years of teaching and how they became whole language teachers but under none of the constraints that we have. They were allowed to be beginners, to have sloppy plans, to try things and have them not work.

I think, even among whole language teachers, there is a notion in the U.S. that you have to pay your dues. You've got to teach the basics for a few years before you're ready to do other things. I think that's because most of us who are whole language teachers have experienced that our lesson plans had better be twice as organized and twice as spelled out and our evaluation system had better be more highly documented because we're under a lot of scrutiny. We weren't allowed to be beginners in whole language. We aren't given the kind of leeway that teachers who are using teacher's manuals and basal materials enjoy. They can just note in the plan book that they're teaching page 67 in the social studies book.

So everything has to be highly organized and documented. I think in that kind of environment it's almost impossible to be a whole language teacher *and* a beginning teacher.

YETTA: As you talk, it reminds me that this is how we treat kids in our schools. We don't let kids be beginners at reading and writing. From the very start their handwriting has to be perfect, their spelling has to be correct, and their form has to be appropriate to whatever the conventional criteria are. What is it about our culture that doesn't allow people to develop?

TOBY: I was just thinking of Ken's warning that we have to stop thinking of children as defective little adults. I've also been thinking about why there is a perception that teachers don't want to develop—they just want to know what to do on Monday morning. I think that partly it's because our profession has been dominated by women for a long time and I really think it relates to how women are controlled in this society and the ways that administrators try to control teachers. Knowledgeable and creative teachers are hard to control; administrators can't always figure out exactly where they should be and what they should be doing.

YETTA: Why do you think school systems have difficulty dealing with innovative teachers?

TOBY: When you've got an innovative program, they can't evaluate it by looking at a lesson plan sheet. I don't write up thirty lesson plans and put them on a sheet of paper for a principal. So that means the administrator has to come into the classroom and see what's going on. And that's a different role for administrators, even though, historically, they were supposed to be principal-teachers who were integrated with everything going on in the school and served in a rotating position. Well, we don't have those kinds of administrators anymore, generally.

Bringing the Classroom into the Real World

In Toby's whole language classroom, she deals with the real issues of growing up in urban America as part of the curriculum. Sometimes the kids find confirmation in their own lives and carry classroom insights into their life experiences.

TOBY: Something happened today that I should talk about. Allen, one of the seventh-grade boys who was in our writing program last year, came up to me. We had been watching *Eyes on the Prize*, a video documentary, part of our thematic unit on the struggle for equal rights.

He came down the hall at 8:15 when I was unlocking my door saying, "Mrs. Curry, you'll never guess what happened to me yesterday. I felt like one of the kids in Little Rock Central High back in 1954." He had gone yesterday to St. Claire Shores, a white suburb, with a Catholic youth organization. He and Laquida, his cousin, were the only two black kids among about four hundred students, and some kids harassed them.

DEBI: He was able to put it into historical perspective.

TOBY: He saw the relationship of his experience to the integration of Little Rock Central High School. He said Laquida was so upset that she didn't come to school. Racism is alive and well in St. Claire Shores. I said, "I think we need to at least write the press. Maybe we can get a newspaper reporter to interview you. Ask your mother how she would feel about that."

YETTA: People believe that these things don't happen—or that minority group members exaggerate them—because they've never been in a situation like this, never felt the fear. These kids have family histories of racism that they have heard about, and that extends the fear. That's a part of socialization to your own culture and group.

DEBI: I had a good, sensitive student teacher, and he was using the B'nai Brith prejudice reduction program called A World of Difference with the kids. One day he asked them if America is living up to its American dream. A lot of the black kids began to tell stories about situations in which they were treated in a racist way, and he couldn't accept what they were telling him. He kept saying, "Well, I never saw that." And he lost all of his teacher objectivity. It wasn't his experience, so he couldn't imagine that in this day and age, people are really treated that way.

YETTA: So how do you use writing and reading to get at these real-life politics?

TOBY: I told Allen, "We need to do something about this, and you should at least consider writing a letter to the *Detroit Free Press.*" He said, "Well, what about the *Michigan Chronicle?*" I said, "That would be fine, but they've got a predominantly black leadership."

YETTA: Tell me how you got involved with the *Michigan Chronicle.* That's a power issue too, because your kids now have some sense that their writing can affect the real world.

TOBY: The *Chronicle* did a piece on our summer writing program, and I met the managing editor, Danton Wilson. We got into a discussion about reading and writing, and as a professional writer he was telling how schools so often kill writing for children. He said the reason he became a writer is because he had a fifth-grade teacher who was special.

I told him about the Dewey Center, what it was like and what kind of writing activities we do, and he came to my classroom and let the kids interview him. He told them that if they would like to write some columns and submit them to the *Chronicle,* he would consider publishing them. All of a sudden, the kids figured they had a voice—they could talk and write about their experiences and investigations. So we started out by interviewing some teachers in the building.

They've finished one column that they wrote about the school and another about the man behind the mayor, the deputy mayor of Detroit. We also interviewed Rose Bell, a senior citizen who started an organization called United Neighbors years ago and has organized a tremendous number of community events. She has a program for unwed mothers, gets layettes and supplies for newborn babies, and helps young girls having babies get on their feet. She has a very sympathetic style with kids.

DEBI: The message that all the people who have come in from the community have given the kids is that it's not only important, it's *essential* that you be involved in your community. It's the responsibility of the community to change the community. A neighborhood like the Jefferies Public Housing Project can't blame all the problems on the residents, but what they are saying is that if the residents got together and got organized, the community would not be like it is.

One of the kids asked Rose Bell, "Isn't it dangerous to be a community organizer?" And she said, "Yes, it is dangerous." But she said it's dangerous walking out of your door in this neighborhood. And she told the kids that people have said that they were afraid for her because these people are serious, these drug pushers. This is a dangerous situation, but even so, kids should get organized, get involved, and help change their community.

Whole Language for Minority Kids

Recently, there have been suggestions that whole language is really only effective for middle-class white kids. Toby and Debi reject that on the basis of personal experience.

TOBY: When people charge that whole language isn't for minority kids, I can hear the white power structure talking because whole language is so empowering. What do we do with all these minority kids who are angry about the system? If we make them literate, powerful learners, they might make some changes in this culture. We've realized that everybody is a whole language learner. I'm a whole language learner, and every kid I've ever taught is a whole language learner.

DEBI: That isn't to say that all children learn in the same way. Dave Bloome, who was then at the University of Michigan, studied Toby's classroom and other classrooms in our school, looking at multicultural populations. He found that in classrooms where there are choices, children use the cultural patterns that they develop in their homes. So that if they have a style of learning that says, "I want to sit at my desk and learn by myself," they can. And if they have the style of learning that says, "I like to learn with a group around me," they can.

And if they have the style of learning that says, "I like to be in charge," they can find a group to be in charge of. Or if they like to be a follower, they can find someone to follow.

Dave found that in Toby's classroom, some of the kids did most of their work at home and others did all of their work in school and never took anything home. I find similar things in my classroom. I have kids in fourth and fifth grade who do most of their reading at home, avid readers who don't read a lot in school; they're too social. Whole language is more flexible. Classroom structure allows for the divergent learning styles of different cultural groups.

YETTA: Why would middle-class black parents or teachers believe that whole language is not for black kids?

TOBY: I think they would only believe that if they didn't understand whole language. I can't believe that's coming from a knowledge base, where they have really read some research and talked with people and then made that statement.

YETTA: Out of a lack of a knowledge base they hear somebody say that whole language is just taking the desks out and moving the pillows in. And this is comparable to what people said about progressive education in the early part of the century and open education in the sixties and now whole language.

DEBI: Parents need to see that what is going on in the classroom has legitimate reasons and success. Parents see that kids seem to be having a good time; the kids go home and say they played all day, we didn't do reading, we didn't do writing, because it's not the traditional reading and writing they're used to. Many parents feel concerned, but black parents are especially concerned because they feel that if their kids are going to be successful they've got to have a good education, maybe even better than other kids. And their view of what a good education is is based upon their own experience. You work harder, you grind it out and put your mind to it. So their expectation is for drill and practice.

The other issue is, what is the content of the curriculum? Let's not, as whole language teachers, focus so much on process that we forget that content is important. We must address the political issues, the cultural and historical issues that matter and are important to black people. If we don't show our concern, then we're going to lose black parents and other minority parents.

TOBY: When my students did I-Search papers [Macrorie 1984], I tried to give them some range. The sixth-grade curriculum is geography, so I told them to pick any country in the world they'd like to learn more about, become an expert about it, and teach the rest of us.

They'd been so devoid of power over their own learning they couldn't believe that I could trust them to be an expert and teach others about Mexico, about Italy. I heard stuff like, "This is not what I'm used to. I'm used to reading the chapter and answering the questions in the back. I've never done this before."

They didn't know anything about note-taking; lots of them just copied whole sentences. I told them, "You can't trust one author or one book about anything. You need to read a variety of things, to piece together your information and learn that just because it's in a book doesn't make it true."

In the follow-through, one girl, Eboney, had a big influence on the other kids. She decided to do her I-Search on Italy and didn't know what to do for a culminating project. Eventually some decided to publish books, one kid did a picture display, and Allen wrote a play. But Eboney was one of the first to do a book, and she decided to model it after Ann McGovern's series *If You Lived in Colonial Times*. She wrote *If You Lived in Italy* and included a little bit about Italy's art and history and a little bit about the popes. She started to get upset when everybody began copying her. They loved the idea, and I tried to help her see that she was a great model. Kandace wrote *If You Fought in the War of 1812*, and Tameka wrote *If You Traveled the Great West*.

Then they presented their research to the class. We all write each presenter a feedback letter: what we liked, what we thought about the presentation, what we thought worked well, but without any nasty comments. So they all get letters from each classmate, and while we're writing these letters the person that presented is writing a letter to me, letting me know how he or she thinks the presentation went, a little self-evaluation.

DEBI: I want to stress again the notion that you put a child in the role of expert when you tell children they are going to make a presentation. It's a very powerful role. When a kid is presenting anywhere from five to twenty minutes and then says to the class, "Are there any questions?," the child is the expert at that moment, and the talk for the next half-hour or forty-five minutes is all kids' talk. The teacher only asks her own questions or maintains order. It's really interesting.

Curriculum Making

Debi and Toby see themselves as curriculum makers. It isn't that they ignore the state and district curricula. It's that they feel obligated to make the curriculum suit their learners rather than the other way around.

YETTA: It sounds to me like both of you are involved in developing your own curriculum. Now you did mention that you're following the social studies guide.

TOBY: Very generally: just that sixth grade is geography and seventh grade is American history.

YETTA: Do you ever think you're short-changing your kids by not doing what the Detroit Board or the state department of education has suggested?

TOBY: I do *more* than what they suggest, that's the way I look at it—because we use newspapers constantly and I show them videotapes like the *Eyes on the Prize* series and different "Wonderworks" specials.

The State of Michigan and the Detroit Public School Board say that I'm supposed to use only one textbook, but that doesn't have everything in it. A big influence in my seventh grade is black history, and the textbook is short on black history. I do black history all year long.

YETTA: You did worry about that the first year you taught using whole language approaches.

TOBY: The first year I was very worried about it. I even gave a test. I remember they were all writing about different topics in colonial America and we had webs and it was great. Then I panicked and gave them a test to see if they were really learning anything. But I made up something like thirty individual tests.

DEBI: David Bloome was concerned because he felt that some of the students would feel double-crossed, that they didn't quite believe that Toby was really teaching this way. And then if she gave them a test, they would feel, "How could you do this to us? We weren't prepared for this." So we convinced Toby that if she was going to give a test she should at least test what she was teaching. So she gave each of them an individual topic and they had to do a quicky report on this one topic. It was an open book test, they had a time limit, and they did great.

TOBY: It was the last teacher-made test I gave, and that was six years ago.

Power to the Teacher

Teachers and learners can be stripped of their power. But it takes an empowered teacher to help kids discover their power. Toby and Debi share their sense of themselves.

YETTA: Do you feel empowered as a teacher?

TOBY: Yes. It's one of the reasons I don't lust after an administrative position. I think I would have to acquiesce to the higher powers, at least in our district. As a teacher, I can get parents and kids to rally around me if I have to. I feel like I can do things. I have to make certain compromises, but I can still have a strong voice by doing my own research and writing. I have a support group of teachers that I meet with once a month, and the knowledge that I have gained in the last five years—I feel really powerful from that. I've learned a lot about language and reading and how kids learn to read and write, and I can verbalize it. And I feel like I'm getting better at watching kids and learning about them, so I can help their parents understand what I'm seeing.

YETTA: Debi, you're not as positive as Toby all of the time.

DEBI: I'm still waiting for the axe to fall, but I'm ready to fight the battle. I think that's what Toby does when she says she's ready to get people to rally behind her. One of the things that has been empowering for Toby and me is that we're ready to quit these jobs when they're no longer working for us, when we reach the point where there's too much compromise. And in a way it's empowering for me to be prepared to do something else, to feel like I'm teaching in this school because I want to. I don't have to. I'm doing it because it's something I'm dedicated to and not that I'm forced to. What keeps us in Detroit is the feeling that we're making a contribution. The Detroit, Chicago, and New York school systems exist, and they don't disappear because we go to the suburbs to teach or go on to the university.

I don't know if we've talked enough about the positive aspects of teaching in Detroit, and we may sound like missionaries. We can offer a lot, but we get a lot out of working with a diverse cultural group. One of the really positive things is that Detroit is a liberal city and the parents love it when we do black history or civil rights units. We've done fairly radical things, and we've never had complaints from parents.

YETTA: They don't ask you to censor reading materials?

TOBY: They sit there and cry as they hear their kids recite Langston Hughes, or talk about Harriet Tubman. We feel we don't have to compromise our politics. In February, two days after Mandela was released, there was an impromptu march here in Detroit. So I went to the march with my kids. It was Wednesday, a school day. We sent home notes for the parents to sign.

Our little window is getting bigger. My old classroom was my window into the world. I had some influence with two groups every day, and Debi had the same with the fifth grade. And now our window has grown to be our influence on a whole school emerging.

DEBI: We balance our pros against the cons of working in the system in Detroit: the facts of not having very much time, carrying very large loads, having to spend a lot of our own money, not having things like tables, bookshelves, pencils.

YETTA: How do you get journals for journal writing?

TOBY: There is a budget for the school, and because it's a whole language school we're saying to them that we need to budget for lots of paper, lots of notebooks, and we are getting more of those things. And that's been the difference from the other school. If you didn't ask for your composition books at the beginning of the year, they were gone, and tough luck if you wanted to do journals.

The Politics of Compromise

Most of the compromise that Toby and Debi accept now is for the benefit of the kids. They have strong beliefs, and they'll give up a job rather than compromise them. But they know that the kids will still be there if they leave, so they make some compromises to stay with the kids and help them cope with the system.

YETTA: To what degree should a teacher compromise principles?

TOBY: I've been thinking about this. I don't want to hurt kids because of my beliefs. There used to be a test in Detroit, the ABC writing test, and the kids had to write a horrible little paragraph on this standard paragraph form. It was the notorious five-sentence paragraph: topic sentence, three supporting sentences, and a concluding sentence. It's not real writing, but it would get them a passing grade. So I compromised. I taught my kids how to take the test. I told them, "This isn't real writing, but this is how you can write for this test." But I also warned them that they could come up against other teachers who would ask them to write like this.

YETTA: To me, you're demystifying the system for them by being honest with them: there are different genres of writing, and testing is one genre. It's not the writing we do, but it's real world. And certain teachers have different values, and you need to get used to all of us.

TOBY: I'm compromising right now. I'm passing out math sheets for the CAT test, for practice. I picked out the chapters in the math book that they could work on for fractions and other things that will be on this test, and to me that's a compromise. Kandace said, "Isn't there a reading part of this test?" And I said, "Yes, but you guys are reading and writing all the time; we're not going to work on that."

DEBI: I think we're ready to get pretty radical about math, but it isn't a decision that we can make for the child. Toby and I are totally against tests; we're against them because they label children, they dictate curriculum. They're used to evaluate teachers, to track children, to terrify and control parents. And here we are, telling kids you're all capable, you're all wonderful, and then these tests place them on a bell-shaped curve and tell them that they're incompetent.

We decided that our kids are going to do more than those in an economically deprived area are supposed to do. On the other hand, we decided when we make presentations to teachers that we're not going to answer the question "How do your kids do on standardized tests?" We're not going to give credence to testing.

Today kids are harassed, pressured, they're supposed to measure up according to tests. It's such a deficit view. Why do we have a society in which you're not supposed to be creative or innovative? Industrial words are creeping into education; kids are viewed as products, and programs are supposed to be cost-effective. Do we think about that when we raise a baby: I want to make this baby cost-effective with the minimum amount of love, attention, and dollars spent? Do we want our schools to be cost-effective, or do we want to provide the richest environment for our children, human beings who are trying to grow?

If you're a farmer, is it cost-effective to just toss the seeds out into the driest soil and use the least number of people to cultivate them?

YETTA: And yet at the same time, what's interesting about what's happening in business and industry is that they want creative people. They want innovative people, and they're worried that we're producing people who only do what they're told.

TOBY: It costs about $27,000 a year to keep someone in prison; if we could just take that money ahead of time, when they're born, and spend it to educate them. If we had been spending billions of dollars on schools since 1945 instead of the arms race, we'd have a lot better situation now.

DEBI: One thing short funds leads to is oversize classes. I think schools do a lot of things because we're working with ridiculous numbers of students. What parent would invite thirty-four kids to a birthday party? The teacher is not only supposed to entertain the children but teach them. You end up spending a lot of your time managing these kids; you keep them quiet, keep them in rows, and enforce procedures like raising their hands to talk and lining up and marching quietly in the hallways, that you wouldn't have with fewer kids.

YETTA: Any last words on the political nature of literacy, in your classroom, in this country?

TOBY: It's virtually impossible for somebody to tell me and my children what we should be learning. We have to make those decisions ourselves. It has to be something that interests us and that we think is important. The idea that people can create these asinine tests, that paranoid administrators can dictate curriculum to teachers and children, is ridiculous. If I don't like something, I'm not going to be enthusiastic about it in the classroom. If it's not interesting to me and I don't think it's meaningful, I'll convey that to the kids somehow. I can't get up there and lie. So I'm constantly looking for what they're interested in and sharing what I'm interested in and trying to tie it all together in learning about life. There's nothing on a standardized test that says anything about Alex getting up in February and reading a poem in front of the class, a kid who in September said he couldn't read well and thought he couldn't write because he couldn't spell. These are the incidents that I'm evaluating all the time in the classroom.

DEBI: And when Sam finally says to me, "I want to read," and he seeks me out, that's significant. That speaks about trust. In the literacy campaigns of underdeveloped countries, the significant feature is not that literacy is empowering; it's that you cannot have power without literacy in modern society. If you are a reader and a writer, you will have a role in society. Is that true for us?

In order for literacy to be empowering, children have to have a role in the classroom, there has to be a democracy, they have to feel that when they join this literacy club, they will have full rights of membership. The whole language classroom offers kids control, choice, the chance to select the questions and to answer them. They have a block of time to do a variety of things, with a teacher as a resource to help. They also have to have the right to goof off and goof up because they didn't learn how to be responsible. If you give kids the opportunity to be responsible, they are going to fool around sometimes, but they have to have that chance. Kids have to be empowered themselves before they can make literacy and learning a powerful experience.

Reference

Macrorie, Ken. 1984. *Twenty Teachers.* New York: Oxford University Press.

THE SUN DOES NOT SET IN GANADO: BUILDING BRIDGES TO LITERACY ON THE NAVAJO RESERVATION

SIGMUND A. BOLOZ
Ganado Primary School
Ganado, Arizona

*T*he sun does not set in Ganado; it reluctantly surrenders in a quiet explosion of brilliant color. This same determination exists in the Navajo people who inhabit these arid lands and in the educators who work with their children.

By mainstream standards, life on the Navajo Reservation is a struggle. With one of the highest unemployment rates in the country, forty-six percent of the families in this area still do not enjoy running water and thirty-five percent have no access to electricity. Although the lifestyle of most Navajo families has adjusted to the larger culture, the 450 students who attend kindergarten through second grade at Ganado Primary School reflect many of the strong values of their ancestors. Children, particularly those from the most traditional families, take on adult responsibility at an early age. It is not unusual to see primary-age children caring for livestock, supervising their siblings, helping to haul water, or chopping wood.

While an occasional student still enters school speaking no English, and while the home language of most is Navajo, our children increasingly have a functional use of English. The higher the socioeconomic status of the family, the more likely it is that the child will speak fluent English.

It is important to understand the circumstances that surround

94

these students, but it is also critical to note that I work with bright, energetic children. They are similar to youngsters around the world who, regardless of their ability to speak English, love to play, to explore, and to learn.

In my twenty years of experience here, I have found that writing and reading processes make as much sense to the teachers of Navajo children as they do in rural New Hampshire among a mostly Anglo population. Although this is a nonsuburban, nonmainstream setting, we do not offer an impoverished language arts curriculum that emphasizes remediation and basic skills. We work with children who have marvelous ideas and remarkable experiences. They are filled with magnificent stories. The creation of appropriate literacy environments must not be seen as a white bread movement; rather, it should be, regardless of color or race, a requirement for the teachers of all children.

A decade ago, I was assigned as the principal of the primary school in Ganado. Having taught young Navajo children in the area for many years, I knew that our educational community had much to learn about the teaching of writing and reading. The successful experiences that I had had in my classroom became one impetus to the transformation of Ganado Primary School's language arts curriculum from a textbook-dominated to a child-centered program. Over the last decade, the school has received encouraging support. It has been selected as one of Arizona's ten outstanding elementary schools, an Arizona Exemplary Literacy Site, and a National Lead School by the National Council of Teachers of English in their "Centers of Excellence for Students at Risk" program.

Our efforts to inspire children, parents, staff, and administrators continue. Perhaps our location, sixty miles from the nearest off-reservation town, aided our development, for while we watch—with satisfaction—as developmentally appropriate literacy practices begin to gain acceptance across North America, we have had to rely on our own resources to build bridges across the many roadblocks to our growth.

One roadblock has been the traditional, accepted view of literacy teaching. Even on the reservation, parents have told me that they expect their children to read from workbooks and basals, to learn a series of discrete, separate subjects and subskills, and to receive frequent grades. After all, they remind me, textbooks and workbooks were used to instruct them and the teachers.

Another roadblock has been the tendency of educators to use an overabundance of educational terminology. The jargon of our profession can be nonspecific and confusing. It took me a long time to realize that when I spoke about writing or phonics, teachers and parents were often filtering what I said through their prior experience. The term *writing* was as likely to be perceived as handwriting, and a discussion of the value of phonics was as frequently viewed as a debate about the usefulness of worksheets and workbooks as it was a conversation about strategies for helping students develop sound-symbol relationships.

Curriculum manuals have been another roadblock. These encyclopedias abound in all districts and ours is no exception, but they are seldom used to direct teaching or learning. Recently I conducted a survey of several hundred teachers from schools across New Mexico and Arizona. When I asked them what set of standards they based their day-to-day classroom decisions on, their district curriculum manuals came in dead last in usefulness. Knowledge about children and their interests was mentioned as most useful. In fact, most teachers didn't remember seeing their district curriculum guides that year.

Finally, most teachers who teach writing and reading are not literate themselves in the sense that they write and read regularly. This has been perhaps the hardest roadblock to overcome. Would you schedule surgery with a doctor who confessed that his or her knowledge was limited to reading about the operation? Is the education of our children any less important?

As an inhabitant of the reservation, I have learned to appreciate the power of traditions to add order and strength. The Navajo people have embedded within their culture a strong extended family and clan system. These are particularly important to the survival of the individual, because a person seldom finds himself or herself without support. Those who have share. Those who know share. Sharing is fundamental to this culture. While there is a deep respect for the knowledge of the elders, decisions are usually made with tremendous input from all participants. As a principal, I see important parallels in the development of our school. The most important bridge to overcoming our roadblocks was to institutionalize a new set of traditions—in effect, to change the balance of power within the school.

Every school has a culture. Those cultures evolve over time. They dictate what people do and how they should relate to one another. Although a culture has many layers, an outsider can only view a surface level. Cultures do not change quickly.

Ganado Primary School is a multileveled culture. At its center is our attempt to establish fluid, rich approaches to writing and reading. Much as within the Navajo culture, we try to respect the opinions of all stakeholders, to share what we know with each other, to develop a strong focus on what needs to be done, and to do "the right thing."

We began with the creation of the Ganado Learning Arts Development (GLAD) project, which gave us a common identity and a sense of purpose. Since controlling the budget was an administrative responsibility as well as an influential tool in school change, I began offering teachers resources to support the publication of student writing. I assured those who already encouraged writing that if they would produce classroom anthologies, I would ensure bound, mimeographed copies. Writing began to spread. A first-grade teacher wrote:

> After all the frustration, a miracle happened yesterday. One of the girls in my room CLICKED. She started writing and it made so much more sense to her. She's so excited that she's been writing all morning. I'm excited too! Success at last.

In those early years, we published dozens of anthologies, began a school newspaper, established a publication lab, and began calling our schoolwide writing emphasis the GLAD project. A label for the project seemed to build pride and identity and added a schoolwide focus to the work.

As a community, the school board, staff, and parents worked through several needs assessments to examine our school district's mission in relation to community values. From these discussions we adopted a series of statements. The most important described a philosophy:

> Children enter school with a demonstrated ability to learn. They are already developing their sense of curiosity, strong interests, and self-identity. The school must acknowledge and develop these capabilities. Parental and staff participation, a supportive community and school environment, and a strong curriculum integrated with appropriate instructional methods will enhance each child's optimal growth.

Next we developed foundation statements that incorporated a Navajo view of education. We examined research and practice, but we also consulted traditional teachings and the underpinnings of traditional ceremonies, such as the Navajo Beauty Way, for direction. Such ceremonies expressed the duality of the world —every living thing finds its purpose in relation to another—

and stressed the simplicity of the cycles of the day, the seasons, and human life.

As a result of our discussions about the school's mission, we recognized the importance of the communication arts, critical thinking, career direction, social-interpersonal skills, and respect and reverence for the environment and self as the foundations upon which our curriculum should be established. These were supported by the traditional Navajo model of teaching and set the foundation for instruction within the culture and for preparing students for a life after school.

The teachers and I crafted the primary school curriculum in a simple format. Instead of a long list of objectives, we composed a forty-page manual that describes our assumptions about education, the classroom environment, the teacher's role, opportunities that students and teachers should be given, and expected outcomes. This is a teacher's curriculum, one that respects the teacher and is sensitive to the realities of the classroom. We call our system a *meaning-based curriculum* because it begins with the child's natural ability to make sense of the world. Within its framework teachers develop their own approaches as long as the integrity of a child-centered program with meaningful content is maintained. In the writing section of the manual we set goals—for example, "Students will have opportunities to participate in some aspect of the writing process daily, choose their own topics for writing, choose their own forms for writing, spell at their developmental level when writing rough drafts or writing to clarify ideas, share their writing, and receive response from peers and their teachers in small and/or large group settings."

Formalizing a curriculum was a positive step, as was the school board's adoption of our document, but a curriculum does not teach children, nor does it ensure that learning will take place. The staff and I worked together to develop procedures that invited children's engagement with the curriculum. Although there are minimal parameters for planning that all staff must address, we agreed that teachers would develop lessons in a style that met their needs. It is in the narratives that each teacher writes that we discover if the spirit of the curriculum is alive in a classroom.

The narratives are a set of documents in which a teacher describes how he or she will address the curriculum. They are fluid in the sense that teachers may update them as necessary. Here the teacher discusses the organization of the classroom, the format of instruction, how he or she presents the various subjects, and what a visitor might see when the teacher and children are at work. Teachers might also describe their expectations, procedures, evaluation of students, and how they integrate learning across the curriculum.

Teacher evaluations take several forms. Although the district requires that I address a set of competencies in a formal observation and evaluation, I have supplemented the process with techniques that get at the spirit of the teaching-learning process. For instance, I might sit at a table with a group of children as they work through their assignments and then provide the teacher with feedback from my observations of the children and conversations with them. I also make frequent classroom visits to look for trends within the classroom, such as the balance between teacher-directed and child-centered activities.

I try to vary my evaluation techniques to provide the kind of response that is most useful to a particular teacher. One teacher might submit a self-evaluation of his or her literacy strategies, another teacher might suggest that I observe an interesting child across a series of lessons and write a narrative of the child's actions, and still another might want to be videotaped and then watch the tape alone or with me. My goal in evaluating teachers is to bring a particular teacher's decision-making strategies to a conscious level. Much as in a writing conference, we decide together whether this teacher is ready for editing, should continue revising, or needs to develop a stronger focus. In almost all instances, the teacher has an opportunity to set goals in areas where he or she chooses to improve the literacy environment.

Although we have adopted a student portfolio that follows the child throughout the school, and although the parents of kindergartners receive narrative reports, we have struggled with the issue of report cards. In the first and second grades we reduced the number of areas graded on report cards to five: reading, writing, spelling, mathematics, and thematic. No students may receive a *D* or *F*; instead, the teacher indicates an *I* for "improvement needed." We also redesigned the report cards to reflect our definitions of literacy; for instance, the basis for first- and second-grade students' grades in writing is the ability to generate their own topics and ideas, write during writing period, write with fluency, make sense, take risks in spelling, rework their own writing, publish their own work, and share their writing in groups. Teachers attach a curriculum summary of the last six weeks in order to develop a context for the report.

We also take a districtwide writing sample twice a year, which is scored holistically by teachers from all four of the schools. This effort involves the scoring of over 1,600 first- through twelfth-grade writing samples during one weekend immediately following the assessment. The training that the teachers receive, and the thought and discussion involved in scoring papers from all grade levels mixed together, has provided a real focus for articulating a writing curriculum across the four schools within our district. This practice has also enhanced communication among teachers within the four buildings.

An invaluable contribution to the success of our literacy program was the hiring of a full-time instructional resource teacher to be a mentor, demonstration teacher, and colleague to Ganado teachers. She coordinates the curriculum and staff development programs, organizes such schoolwide celebrations as young authors' week, supervises two resource rooms (one of which houses a professional library of over a thousand volumes), and collects multiple sets of children's literature and appropriate supplies to encourage teachers to continue to develop their approaches to reading and writing. She is, in short, a far cry from the traditional version of a curriculum coordinator who sits at a desk passing paper.

Over the past several years our staff meetings evolved from policy and procedural updates into sharing sessions where teachers discuss classroom practice, journal articles, and books of interest. In addition, building committees review curriculum development, but they have also taken over the organization of mini-workshops in their curriculum areas during monthly early-release days for staff development. These, in turn, have expanded into weekend seminars and workshops at which local teachers explore techniques and topics in depth.

I have granted Ganado Primary teachers unlimited release time, and I encourage them to visit each other's classrooms to view colleagues' approaches to writing, literature study, and thematic units. We have also allocated funds to allow teams of teachers to attend regional and national conferences at which literacy development is highlighted. The attendance of teams from various grade levels at these conferences has been incredibly important in cultivating dialogue among teachers and validating current school practices.

In addition, each grade level grouping has release time for our monthly "Eight to Whenever" meetings. These sessions, which begin over breakfast and end whenever we finish, give staff members an opportunity to discuss grade level and schoolwide curriculum issues in depth. Teachers share samples of student work that have resulted from successful practices in a forum that allows sufficient time to hammer out terminology and make plans for the future. Ganado Primary School also established a budget task force of teachers, so that the staff has direct input into the allocation of school funds.

Our summer issues workshops have created another opportunity to define alternatives. The four-day workshops, held at the end of the school year, little resemble curriculum workshops at which teachers design new manuals. Our issues workshops have a limited purpose: to promote dialogue. As a result of one of the summer sessions, we have established a daily uninterrupted block time in which all instructional staff, including me, work with small groups of students for an hour and a half to help facilitate the children's literacy opportunities. The uninterrupted block time has reduced class size and afforded young readers and writers more individual attention. No pull-outs or special classes are allowed during this time, and ancillary staff have become much more responsive to their roles in supporting reading and writing.

A classroom looks much different when I sit at a table where six children are eager to learn than it does when I am looking over a teacher's shoulder. I have learned more about the needs of students, teachers, and classrooms as I rotated to my new assignment each six weeks during the interrupted block time than I have from listening during meetings because I have used the old books, experienced the lack of supplies, been interrupted by the intercom, and endured the lack of maintenance myself.

I have also learned that if a school has a program with the potential to improve the learning of one group of students within a school, then that program should be made available to all the children in the school. And so I have worked with the staff to create a one-program emphasis, eliminate pull-outs, find ways that supplemental federal and state programs can be designed to support a single focus rather than a fragmentary approach, and coordinate materials and budgets.

Our summer issues discussions led to the establishment of the Success Program, in which all special education students within a grade are teamed in one classroom with a group of accelerated students. This diminishes lost passing time, aids in program coordination, and eliminates the unfortunate message that every student receives when a few children are called out to the resource classroom. In the Success classrooms, a regular classroom teacher and a special education teacher work together with a cross section of students to provide an enhanced literacy curriculum. The students no longer seem aware of who has special needs and who is accelerated. The power of the approach was evident to me when, after the first few weeks of school, one of the second-grade students asked, "When do I go to special ed?"

Ganado teachers have extended Navajo ideas of shared governance and made them their own by creating a teacher support group. Called the Greater Reservation Interdisciplinary Network (GRIN), the support group meets during evenings in the homes of staff members. Over the years, through its biannual conferences, GRIN has grown to become a network for teachers, assistants, and administrators from all areas of the reservation who are interested in literacy development.

Our school's staff has also begun a writer's circle that encourages teachers to share their work and to seek out audiences beyond the reservation for their ideas. As a result, many teachers have published poems, articles, and book reviews, and a few have begun to write children's stories and even novels.

Finally, we have worked to increase parent involvement within the school through a series of Rainbow Connection workshops. In these workshops, parents have an opportunity to sharpen parenting skills, better understand our meaning-based curriculum, view samples of student work, and make suggestions for future planning. Teachers and students have found this an effective forum to present classroom projects. We have taken parents into classrooms where they can experience firsthand the benefits of the writing process, literature study, and thematic units and have created forums for discussing invented spelling, the teaching of skills, and ways that parents can encourage their children's literacy development. Perhaps the best reinforcement for the Rainbow Connection workshops was a note we received from one Navajo parent:

> I have learned to care more about my kids. I am trying to read more to them, to play with them, and to communicate more with my kids. Thanks.

Polls of our students' parents indicate continued strong support for our curriculum and for the kinds of experiences that children enjoy in our classrooms. That support has led to flexibility in the use of supplemental funds to create two computer labs, supply computers to every classroom, and develop a Navajo Enrichment class that enhances the native language. Finally, we continue to inform parents of appropriate practices through our district newsletter. We write and distribute numerous simplified reviews of research in the form of literacy development checklists that suggest how they can assist their children at home and what they should expect to find happening in their children's classrooms.

There will always be barriers to school change. No matter where a school is located or what population of children it serves, the principal must be seek to build bridges over the barriers. The principal must lead. The richest, soundest curriculum does not ensure that children will learn and that teachers will teach. The principal must help parents, teachers, and children become responsible for the program and the school. The principal must understand children, teachers, parents, other administrators, and the culture of the school's community. This means getting involved in classrooms and building strong networks of support. And it means that curriculum development in the language arts is never ending. We don't "do writing" one year, "do reading" the next, and then dust off our hands in satisfaction and move on to math.

Ganado Primary School is an elaborate culture, one that has taken a principal, a talented staff, an eager student body, and a supportive community over a decade to develop. Its underpinnings are our hard work and our assumptions about learning and teaching. We have chosen to allow children to participate in their own education, and we have presented writing and reading processes as inseparable components. These are not white bread staples belonging only on the classroom tables of rural New Hampshire.

As I watch the sun surrender over Ganado, I think I understand the reverence that this traditional people has for all things. The quiet explosion of color offers hope for all people, but especially for the children.

A Guest Essay
LEARNING LITERACY
LESSONS

PATRICK SHANNON
Pennsylvania State University

According to Harste, Woodward, and Burke (1984), educators can learn literacy lessons from the stories teachers tell about children's uses of written language. They argue that descriptions and analyses of what children are trying to do with written texts should direct educators' attempts to develop environments that support literacy. Theirs is a powerful perspective, one that places the power of theory building and the responsibility for literacy development in the hands, hearts, and heads of lesson participants—teachers and students. Language stories should yield literacy lessons.

Recently some concerned citizens have written publicly to criticize teachers, schools, and state officials for considering whole language philosophies. Their letters to the editor, editorials, magazine and newspaper articles, and subsequent lobbying efforts have influenced state and federal legislators' speeches, policy statements, and legislative amendments. Their writings appear in print and at school meetings from Maine to Arizona, from Montana to Florida, and from California to Washington, D.C. More than just attempting to discredit whole language, these people argue that early, systematic phonics is the only scientific, practical, and moral method of teaching anyone to read and write.

I believe educators of all philosophical convictions can learn valuable literacy lessons (and perhaps political ones, too) from the language stories in and around this public writing. By looking at the intent as well as the content of their efforts, educators can draw conclusions about how we might ourselves use literacy to participate in the debate about how literacy should be taught.

Letters to the Editor

Letters to the editor are an important tradition in civic writing (Stotsky 1986). Citizens express themselves in response to particular articles and editorials, or to a newspaper's lack of coverage of specific topics or events. Most often the author is a local citizen providing a view different from those expressed in the newspaper. In the case of schools or districts considering whole language alternatives, however, this is not always the case. Letters from across the country frequently appear on local opinion pages to defend intensive phonics or to lampoon alternatives. These letters do not pull their punches.

For example, Patrick Groff, a retired education professor from San Diego, exchanged a series of letters in a Maine paper, the *Boothbay Register*, with Nancie Atwell, a former Boothbay teacher. Groff's first letter, published on October 26, 1989, comments on Atwell's withdrawal eighteen months earlier of a proposal to assist local teachers in using children's literature as the foundation for their literacy lessons because some members of the school board had made it clear that they thought the teachers incapable of delivering such a program. Groff begins: "The reluctance of the Boothbay School Committee in 1988 to accept $50,000 in materials and services offered as an inducement to establish a 'whole language' program of literacy development in its schools has come to my attention." He goes on to comment that the school committee is "wise" to be reluctant because "the idology [*sic*] held about reading instruction by WL advocates like Ms. Atwell have [*sic*] been demolished in large part by the scientific data on this teaching." After a response from Atwell in which she wondered aloud why Groff was writing so late from so far away on a matter no longer under consideration, Groff again responded (January 4, 1990) with "congratulations" for "the courageous stand of Committee members" against "Atwell's dubious scheme." In this second letter, Groff aligns himself with Marilyn Adams's (1990) *Beginning to Read*, which he cites as *Phonics and Beginning Reading Instruction* with a 1989 publication date, and adds that he writes to distant local newspapers because "national educational journals at present will not print negative criticisms of the WL suppositions."

A similar letter from Marshall Kaminsky, an educator from San Francisco, appeared in the *News-Argus* in Lewiston, Montana (January 6, 1988), criticizing the local school district's cross-grade reading program. Kaminsky took exception to the journalist's positive tone in the original article about the program and wrote that "it was really a story about dismal failure." According to Kaminsky, fifth graders, who worked in the project with high school students, shouldn't need help with their reading because "children should be able to read, spell, and comprehend every word in the *Declaration of Independence* by the end of second grade." The reason for the failure was that Lewiston teachers were using "the useless and destructive look-say or the whole language method" instead of intensive phonics, "the only reading instructional method that works. . . . It worked for our forefathers and even our current president [Reagan]."

Articles and Editorials

Newspaper and magazine articles about reading instruction are rare. Most often, they touch on celebrity initiatives (Mrs. Bush's efforts to fight illiteracy) or recount standardized test scores for local districts or the state. Because these media rarely consider reading, it warrants careful consideration when they do.

In July 1989, *The New American*, "a spokesman for activities of the American Defense Fund concentrating in content upon internal security matters vital to your well being," published an article by William Jasper entitled "Half-taught with Whole Language." Jasper charged that whole language is a "top-down campaign devised and promoted by the professional 'reading wreckers' of the International Reading Association." Citing Marian Hynds, the President of the Reading Reform Foundation, Jasper reports that "whole language is a revised version of the old look-say, sight word method which is basically responsible for the decline of literacy and the increase in reading disabilities in America." He continues: "Because of this teaching, millions of students develop the well-known symptoms of dyslexia, that dreaded learning disability that condemns capable, bright students to lives of mediocrity."

On August 23, 1989, the *Christian Science Monitor* published an opinion piece by Martha Brown, Illinois co-chairperson of the Reading Reform Foundation, that associates whole language learning ("a method adopted by thousands of schools in the '80s") with a decline in Scholastic Aptitude Test scores and an increase in the number of school dropouts. According to Brown, the problem is so severe that "even in upper middle class districts 25 to 30 percent of public elementary students [*sic*] need remedial help." To the typical list of whole language advocates— education professors, professional journals, and professional organizations—Brown adds unions. At the end of her piece she calls for parents "to bring sense (phonics) back into the classroom before whole language becomes the epitaph for education reform."

Newsletters

"The purpose of [the *Blumenfeld Education Letter*] is to provide knowledge for parents and educators who want to save the children of America from the destructive forces that endanger them. Our children in the public schools are at grave risk in 4 ways: academically, spiritually, morally, and physically—and only a well-informed public will be able to reduce those risks." Editor (and sole author) Samuel Blumenfeld devoted the March 1989 issue of his *Letter* to "The Whole Language Fraud." In this issue he presents an overview of whole language and offers commentary on the work of Kenneth Goodman (someone who treats "English as if it were Chinese"), the International Reading Association ("virtually the entire reading establishment . . . are [*sic*] controlled by proponents of look-say and whole language"), and the Marie Carbo/Jeanne Chall exchange about Chall's *Learning to Read* (1967) ("Bravo, Professor Chall"). Blumenfeld extends the blame for the "problems of dyslexia and functional illiteracy," however, to include elementary school teachers—"many of [whom] were themselves taught to read by look-say and are semiliterate."

Blumenfeld gives special attention to Francie Alexander, Associate State Superintendent for California. First he reminds his readers that Alexander announced the California Language Arts Initiative toward literature-based literacy programs and then quotes her statement to the press about the impact of the California Board of Education's unanimous approval of a policy to strengthen the teaching of evolution. Blumenfeld draws two conclusions: "Between evolution and whole language, there is no telling what kind of damage will be done to the minds and souls of the children of California . . . and how can anyone have confidence in American public education when the 'experts' in charge exhibit such ignorance, arrogance, and evil intent."

The U.S. *Congressional Record*

On October 23, 1989, Congressman Joseph Brennan of Maine read a letter from the *Camden Herald* into the *Congressional Record*. The letter, published in the Camden paper on July 6, 1989, was written by Charlotte Iserbyt, an employee of the Department of Education during the Reagan administration. Brennan said he must read Iserbyt's letter to Congress "for the sake of our Nation's economic, political, and social prosperity." The following are selected quotes from the *Congressional Record*.

> Is the failure to teach our children to read and write not the most important civil rights issue facing our nation today? Shouldn't we attack this civil rights problem with at least the same vigor we attacked racial discrimination in our society?
>
> Whole language-look say method of reading instruction must be stopped dead in its tracks if we truly want to cure the nation's illiteracy problems. . . .
>
> The reason for our nation's illiteracy is that the social engineers and so called reading specialists in the International Reading Association have for the past 60 years been busily at work changing the methods of reading instruction from the tried and true intensive phonics to look-say/whole language.
>
> Because unbeknownst to them, the deindustrialization of America, with its accompanying transfer of millions of American jobs overseas, has allowed the social change agents to redefine literacy and to call for new teaching methods, such as whole language and the use of elementary students of calculators [*sic*], better suited to the needs of an information/service oriented society.
>
> Write your congressman and ask them [*sic*] to put a hold on the new NAEP reading test, scheduled for administration in 1990, pending an investigation of its alignment to a single discredited method of reading instruction, whole language. Nonpartisan citizen action on this extremely important civil rights issue is vital for the survival of our free society.

U.S. Senate Policy Statement

Senator William Armstrong of Colorado issued a report on September 13, 1989, entitled "Illiteracy: An Incurable Disease or Educational Malpractice?" as the Senate Republican policy position on reading instruction. The report seeks to provide a comprehensive analysis of early reading instruction, and it offers much of the same criticism of reading experts, professional organizations, and publishers as Groff, Blumenfeld, and other critics. In fact, some of the text of the report is identical to the *Blumenfeld Educational Letter*. Beyond the similarities, Armstrong reports that "historically, all American school children were taught to read. . . . It seldom, if ever, occurred to teachers to give children word lists to read, or to make beginning readers memorize whole stories as today's proponents of the whole language approach recommend . . . Frank Smith, Kenneth Goodman, and Edmund Huey, all well-known, vociferous, dedicated, dogmatic enemies of early intensive teaching of phonics."

After offering an endorsement of the Reading Reform Foundation, a nonprofit association developed for the promotion of phonics instruction in American schools, Armstrong provides a cost analysis of federal literacy programs from the 1960s to the present (which he estimates at $63 billion) and makes four recommendations. First, "there should be a moritorium on the establishment of new federal programs to prevent illiteracy, until an assessment is conducted to determine the effectiveness of those programs already in existence." Second, the study of beginning reading that Congress approved in 1986 (P.L. 99-425, Sec. 901) should be conducted, complete with cost/benefit analyses of all commercial programs and methods. Third, "in some cases the federal government provides funds directly for reading instruction (prisons, military, job training, Chapter 1, bilingual programs, etc.) . . . in these cases, teachers should be required to be trained in intensive systematic phonics." Fourth, "governors should be encouraged to propose state legislation requiring teachers to be taught intensive systematic phonics as part of their training to teach in public schools."

The National Literacy Act of 1989

On February 6, 1990, the U.S. Senate passed legislation (S 1310), which established procedures to coordinate federal literacy programs, increase workplace and job training literacy programs, establish and strengthen family intervention programs for literacy, distribute books to families and agencies, and develop student and public literacy volunteer programs. According to Senator Paul Simon of Illinois, the act's primary sponsor, "As a nation, I believe that we must ensure that all those who need literacy services will receive them—without being subjected to a waiting list, inaccurate assessments, overcrowded classrooms, or inferior programs taught by poorly trained adult educators. The

National Literacy Act of 1989 is intended to achieve these objectives" (*Congressional Record*, February 5, 1990, p. S 730). The act received rhetorical support from many senators, who linked illiteracy with the economic, social, and political collapse of American society.

Five amendments to the act were proposed, including requests for changes that would allow funding for Parent as Teacher programs, literacy assistance for commercial truckdrivers, and Native American Even Start grants. Senator Armstrong of Colorado presented two amendments. The first was to include at least one classroom teacher ("whose expertise on 'what works' in the classroom will be invaluable") on state literacy councils, a provision of Title 1 of the act. In support of this amendment, Armstrong offered four sentences. But for his second amendment, which he labeled "reading instruction in phonics," he offered selected references from research reports, a selected list of phonics programs, reports of two school districts using phonics, and the entire Senate Republican Policy Statement mentioned above. He stated that "for too long we have been unwilling to deal with the root cause of the problem of illiteracy in America and that is the flawed methods we have used to teach our children to read" (p. S 738). "If we apply the recommendation of the years of research and retrain our classroom teachers, we can eliminate illiteracy before the year 2000 (p. S 739)." In his press release of February 6, 1990, Senator Armstrong reports that because of his amendment, federal money can "be spent to train teachers in phonics instruction."

The Content of These Language Stories

Although, typically, Harste, Woodward, and Burke do not comment on the content of the stories their young informants tell, I would be remiss if I overlooked the content of these documents in order to analyze only the intent, style, and process with which these writers made their points. I will ignore the more extreme statements of criticism (school teachers are semiliterate), comparison (Goodman, Smith, and Huey are more dogmatic in their beliefs than Chall, Adams, and Flesch in theirs), and praise (the courageous stand of school board members who champion intensive phonics), because such statements do not further the debate on literacy and literacy education. But I will make brief comments on statements about whole language, phonics, and the accused advocates of whole language, because these are important parts of the debate.

Even casual readers of professional journals should recognize inaccuracies in the statements about whole language philosophies. As Altwerger, Edelsky, and Flores (1987) explain, the great debate between look-say and phonics is over word recognition, not reading. A whole language view of reading is "not one of getting words but of constructing meaning" (p. 148) by using graphophonic, syntactic, semantic, and pragmatic cues in the text and the context of the reading. Treating whole language philosophies and look-say as synonomous is a distortion of the facts.

In addition, there is considerable evidence that methods derived from whole language philosophies *are* effective with young children (Pinnell, Fried, and Estice 1990; Winter and Rouse 1990) and for entire populations (Guthrie 1981). Although there is evidence that suggests that instructional methods affect how children learn, I know of no evidence that connects teachers applying whole language philosophies to the development of learning disabilities or dyslexia. Finally, the association of whole language and evolution presents a curious problem in logic. If Blumenfeld believes that whole language should be rejected because it is unscientific, then on what basis should evolution be rejected?

Many of the statements made in favor of phonics are historic inaccuracies and scientific exaggerations. Blaise Pascal did not invent alphabetic phonics as Senator Armstrong claims in his Senate position paper; the method predates him by many centuries (Mathews 1966). Before the twentieth century, not all students learned to read, word and syllable lists *were* featured in early phonics textbooks, and memorization and drill were the primary means of learning at school (Finkelstein 1971; Smith 1987). There were no "good old days" when all Americans were literate—not even in the upper and middle classes, about which Brown worries. During a public meeting at the 1990 International Reading Association Convention, Marilyn Adams, who is cited extensively in many of the pro-phonics documents, stated that "the Armstrong, Blumenfeld, and Brennan reports simplify the arguments about reading and overstate the case for phonics. . . . I never said that the debate [about early reading instruction] is over or that every student needed phonics instruction. I did not say or write that." Finally, it is misleading at best (dishonest at worst) for Senator Armstrong to say that a switch to intensive phonics would eliminate illiteracy in America by the year 2000 (see Kozol 1985, upon whose work the National Literacy Act is based). Moreover, it is dishonest to imply that literacy will necessarily bring employment and prosperity since there are not enough jobs for every illiterate American.

In many of these documents the critics imply that someone, some group, or something is preventing intensive phonics instruction from being taught in schools. The International Reading Association is a favorite target, and the National Assessment of Educational Progress a new one. The IRA does make considerable amounts of money from its association with textbook publishers, but this revenue would not disappear even if all classroom teachers switched to phonics. As is obvious, publishers will produce whatever materials bring them profit. They have demonstrated the ability over the last several decades to repackage their wares (Durkin 1987), and they will continue to do business with the IRA because it brings large numbers of teachers together. The writers' claim that economics explains IRA bias lacks credibility.

The argument against the NAEP is just as spurious. In fact, the Reading Commission of the National Council of Teachers of English, of which I am a Director, refused to participate in the national testing project because they thought the NAEP committee lacked effective advocates of positions other than intensive phonics. They feared that the NAEP tests would lead to a national curriculum based on intensive, systematic phonics. And according to the *Congressional Record* of February 5, 1990, Senator Simon objected to Senator Armstrong's original amendment for phonics instruction because it was intended to establish just such a curriculum. Despite Senator Armstrong's claims, the final wording of his amendment included many alternatives to phonics for teaching reading.

Literacy Lessons

What can educators learn from these stories? These documents represent an excellent example of how a group interested in literacy has used effective political writing to promote its beliefs. And they have been successful in spreading the word. Perhaps the most distinguishing feature of their work is the obvious coordinated effort behind it: How else would national letters come to local newspapers? At each level, from local newspapers to the

Senate floor, there is a singularity of message and method. I don't see the coordination as a conspiracy, but rather as a confederation of like-minded citizens who seek to change reading instruction in public schools by using their literacy as it is intended to be used—to make a difference in their lives. I think there is much here for literacy educators to learn.

First, these writers don't just talk among themselves, as literacy educators at every level often do. Although it is clear from cross-citation that they communicate with each other, they recognize that teachers and school administrators do not make decisions about reading instruction by themselves. Accordingly, the writers have broadened the audience for their writing. They address parents and taxpayers in order to persuade them to accept their viewpoint and to act on their behalf in local schools and districts. They attempt to gain the ear of school board members in order to get their issues on the board's agenda and keep them there. And they follow the money and power of local, state, and federal elected officials.

Second, these writers have increased the number of outlets for their work. They send letters of support and condemnation to local newspapers, national magazines, school boards, business executives, and members of government. They write articles for some of these same sources and for hand-to-hand circulation among local support groups. They also write policy statements for local candidates for office as well as for state and federal legislators. Lately the *Congressional Record* seems to be a favorite outlet, conveying immediate legitimacy to their position.

Third, the simple, plain style of these documents is effective. Sentences are clear declarations of the benefits of the author's position and the liabilities of all others. Although these writers frequently refer to science, they use none of the jargon and very little of the qualifications and explanation of procedures that often accompany scientific reports. Rather, they blend personal and case-study anecdotes with the emotional appeal of a tragedy reversed. Most effective is their effort to present themselves as the persecuted underdog populists fighting against big business, special interest groups, big government, and intellectuals.

Fourth, the timing of their writing is instructive. These writers are proactive in their efforts to get their message across when literacy education is not on local, state, or national agendas. Then they write to ask various audiences why they are not concerned about this "neglected civil right" or to alert those who have already accepted their position to possible threats on the horizon.

These writers react quickly to such threats when they do occur, as the Iserbyt letter about NAEP attests. Finally, they are relentless in their efforts, as the Groff-Atwell exchange in the *Boothbay Register* demonstrates. Even when the threat is gone, the writing comes to ensure that it will not return.

Fifth, these writers extend the context usually associated with discussions about literacy education. They explain how their position is not just better for individuals, or even children in general. Rather, their position is important for society at large. Despite oversimplification, distortion, and hyperbole, they attempt to articulate an economic and political argument for why literacy is important and why their vision of literacy education will improve life in America. Since this is at least part of the reason for schooling, this kind of rhetoric and logic is important in gaining the attention, if not the support, of those not directly involved in education. These writers offer their audience a reason to believe in their cause.

To learn the literacy lessons from these stories, we must follow Harste, Woodward, and Burke's lead and separate story content from literacy process. If we do, the lessons show us what literacy and democracy are all about. They teach us that literacy can serve real purposes beyond momentary pleasure or getting on with the functions of our lives. They demonstrate that through reading and writing, individuals can make their voices heard by those who rarely listen and affect society in ways they believe appropriate. And while some may not appreciate the message they deliver, they are engaged in a legitimate and, from a literacy educator's standpoint, admirable democratic tradition, one in which we all might participate. We have their invitation.

References

Adams, Marilyn. 1990. *Beginning to Read: Thinking and Learning About Print.* Cambridge, MA: MIT Press.

Altwerger, Bess; Carol Edelsky; and Barbara Flores. 1987. "Whole Language: What's New." *Reading Teacher* 41:144–54.

Armstrong, William. 1989. *Illiteracy: An Incurable Disease or Educational Malpractice?* Washington, D.C.: U.S. Senate Republican Policy Committee.

Atwell, Nancie. 1989. Letter to the Editor. *Boothbay* [ME] *Register*, November 2.

Blumenfeld, Samuel. 1989. "The Whole Language Fraud." *Blumenfeld Education Letter* 4 (3):1–8.

Brown, Martha. 1989. "The Basics of School Reform." *Christian Science Monitor,* August 23.

Chall, Jean. 1967. *Learning to Read: The Great Debate.* New York: McGraw Hill.

Congressional Record. 1989. "Teaching Our Children to Read." October 23:E3517–E3519.

———. 1990. "The National Literacy Act." February 5:S730–S741.

Durkin, Dolores. 1987. "Influences on Basal Reading Programs." *Elementary School Journal* 87:331–41.

Finkelstein, Barbara. 1971. "Governing the Young: Teachers' Behaviors in American Primary Schools, 1820–1880." Ph.D. diss., Teachers College, Columbia University.

Groff, Patrick. 1989. Letter to the Editor. *Boothbay* [ME] *Register,* October 29.

———. 1990. Letter to the Editor. *Boothbay* [ME] *Register,* January 4.

Guthrie, John. 1981. "Reading in New Zealand: Achievement and Volume." *Reading Research Quarterly* 17:6–27.

Harste, Jerome C.; Virginia A. Woodward; and Carolyn Burke. 1984. *Language Stories and Literacy Lessons.* Portsmouth, NH: Heinemann.

Iserbyt, Charlotte. 1989. Letter to the Editor. *Camden* [ME] *Herald,* July 6.

Jasper, William. 1989. "Half-taught with 'Whole Language.' " *The New American,* July 3.

Kaminsky, Marshall. 1988. Letter to the Editor. *Lewiston* [MT] *News Argus,* January 6.

Kozol, Jonathan. 1985. *Illiterate America.* Garden City, NY: Anchor.

Mathews, Mitford. 1966. *Teaching to Read.* Chicago: University of Chicago Press.

Pinnell, Gay; Marian Fried; and Rose Estice. 1990. "Reading Recovery: Learning How to Make a Difference." *Reading Teacher* 43:282–95.

Smith, Nila B. 1987. *American Reading Instruction,* 3d ed. Newark, DE: International Reading Association.

Stotsky, Sandra. 1986. "Civic Writing: The Unexamined Component of Civic Literacy." Paper presented at the 1986 National Reading Conference, Austin, TX, December.

Winter, Mildred, and Joy Rouse. 1990. "Fostering Intergenerational Literacy: The Missouri Parents as Teachers Program." *Reading Teacher* 43:382–87.

"CHANGE THE WORD SCREW ON PAGE 42"

ED KENNEY
Ranier High School
Ranier, Washington

I scanned the Macintosh screen one more time, checking for any typos, any *lies* lying low, any *lays* lying in wait. Did other rapid readers have such a devil of a time proofreading? I'd have to ask around. With a little luck, I would be done proofing all ninety-two pages and out of the school building before midnight. Two nights earlier one of the local police had burst in late at night with his gun raised and gripped in both hands, scaring the semicolons out of me.

But the effects of rapid reading on accurate proofreading, and the theatrical behavior of rural policemen, weren't my number one concerns right now. I wondered if this book would ever see the light of day. If it didn't, it wouldn't be for lack of effort. I'd spent the fall and early winter months hunting down essays, poems, and stories for a ten-year retrospective of student writing called *Children of the 80's.* I had already set aside several hundred memorable pieces before receiving a grant to pursue the project, and conversations with mothers, brothers, uncles, and grandmothers of eighties children produced a few hundred more. One of the hardest jobs had been selecting only ninety from over a thousand pages of interesting writing. I had managed to include pieces from seventy different students, but that variety came at a price. Stories longer than eight pages had to be left out. Save them for another book? Sure. I'd be lucky to have a job once this project was finished.

But tonight things were going well. I'd never get used to the whining pulse of the huge library fluorescents way above my head, and the radio wasn't picking up the Mariners-Athletics game being played seventy miles north of this small logging community, but I was on page 81 and moving quickly. Some nights hadn't been this productive, particularly during the selection process. Some nights . . . I just stared at what I had typed, remembering how the piece had evolved. There were so many stories behind the written stories. Most had happy endings, but a few did not. In some pieces you didn't have to look too far beneath the surface to see child abuse, near-suicides, the effects of alcoholism, or even incest; in other pieces only the writer, a few close friends, and a teacher might be able to perceive the calm resolve taken by a student after an important decision or, perhaps, the message in code to a loved one. One piece reminded me of the time a musician came to class with a van full of synthesizers, mixers, and video equipment to talk about his composing process. He played music he had produced for television shows and commercials to a fascinated young audience, and one boy stayed around to help carry the equipment back to the van. I can still see Mike reverently handling the Yamaha DX-7 and asking perceptive questions. New life seemed to flow into his school activities after that. He signed up for drama class, began collecting sound equipment, and helped start a school Sound Club. Then he began earning gas money as a traveling DJ. Unfortunately, it was a car accident late at night that put his name into bold newspaper print.

In other pieces it wasn't the tragedy or personal drama that got my attention. The mimicry and parody of famous authors' styles reminded me of when I'd first introduced each of the writers in class, and the many poems and essays about the computer age pinpointed exactly the year that personal computers had come to our school. Another thing I could clearly see was that the writing in the last half of the decade was better than that in the first half. And there was certainly more of it. Had the recent growth in our community made the difference? More and more of our students now are not loggers' sons and daughters but the children of government workers commuting to the state capital. Or was the difference to be found in the stability our school had settled into after six years with seven different principals? Had I become a better writing teacher? Maybe all of the above.

But on this particular night I wasn't letting the nostalgia warm and paralyze me. I wasn't thinking about the three student writers who had died, or about my closest teacher friends, who had left the school during its unstable years. I was "on task" and the task was this: to print two hundred copies of *Children of the 80's* before an ad hoc committee convened by the principal killed the project. I suspected that one noncontroversial method of execution might be to delay the publication date two more weeks, until the end of the school year.

Finally, I reached the ninety-second page. I knew my hurried proofreading had not uncovered all the spelling errors, and I couldn't even find where several inappropriate *lays* were lying . . . or had lain . . . or were about to lie, but as one of the about-to-be-published students had written, "I was on a mission." I moved down the computer menu to PRINT, and our school Laserwriter began to roll out forty-six legal-sized facing pages. The janitor had already left and my eyes were blurring as I scanned the graphics and type of each page before taping it alongside three others on the printing master. The poetry slowed me down. It was nearly impossible to ignore the sound and rhythm pulsing beneath the larger typefaces. Even now, the magical expression of truth in some of these pieces thrilled me.

Later, much later, the copier sent out its nine thousand two hundredth double-sided copy . . . and survived. It didn't sound the same, and neither did I, and it was long after midnight, and I had used up every copy allowed on every teacher's code number I could remember. I assembled one sample copy and attached the striking four-color cover to it with temporary staples. I guess I had to feel that *Children of the 80's* was real.

The next day I was scheduled to meet with the principal and the two parents on the ad hoc committee he had formed because, as he said, he "didn't feel comfortable censoring the book by himself." One parent was chosen because she was a member of a local book club and the other because she had objected to the school's state-mandated AIDS curriculum and to the uniform her ninth-grade daughter would be wearing on the volleyball team. This was the day that they would be making their recommendations about what should be done with "the book."

I had decided to listen politely to their comments but not to do anything that would give any validity to the formation of this committee or to its process or mission or recommendations. Washington State, along with its sister coastal states, has had more documented cases of censorship than any other region of the country, so there were plenty of places I could go for advice. I spoke with the state Coalition Against Censorship, the ACLU, our local teacher's union, and numerous teachers. I learned that most recent censorship attempts, like this one, originated within the school itself and that the Supreme Court's recent Hazelwood decision had given greater freedom to school administrators in this area. Not surprisingly, two other Supreme Court decisions seemed to restrict this freedom. And state regulations specified how "instructional materials committees" were to be formed. Clearly, one possible result of the meeting today was that lawyers would spend a year in court deciding the fate of *Children of the 80's.* I didn't think there would be much interest left in the book if it came out a year late. There might not be much of my writing program left either.

Yes, I would need to think about strategy. But I kept thinking *why?* Why had the principal responded to the students' writing in this manner and at this time? Starting back in October I had shown him pieces of writing as I tentatively selected them for the book. In fact, since the day he was hired I had painstakingly initiated discussion, often in writing, about any classroom issue that I thought might concern him. He seemed uncomfortable in my classroom and rarely visited it, though I continued to invite him. I usually went to him instead and frequently brought student writing with me. What seemed to interest him as I was preparing the publication were the pieces produced by "marginal" students, some of whom weren't passing English courses. He appeared surprised at the range of such students' vocabulary. Never once did he say that a certain piece was unsuitable for publication. He was well aware that the conditions of my grant specified the use of *Children of the 80's* in class as "instructional material."

And then, late in the year, just as my students were finishing a production of *West Side Story,* he decided that censorship was in order and the week I had set aside to produce the book evaporated. I thought about all this as I finished classes and found a home for student writing in my leather satchel. I remembered the "small world" irony of walking out of a showing of *Dead Poets Society* in Colorado the summer before and running smack dab into our principal, fourteen hundred miles away from home. After the initial astonishment and small talk I asked him how he liked the movie and he smiled, declining comment. I realized there was a lot I didn't know about our principal, and that this storm had been brewing for a long time, and I wondered what it was like for my sister teaching in a large school district completely committed to reading and writing workshops.

When my classes were over for the day, I walked into the principal's office and said hello to the two parents. I remembered another principal's office in another school I'd been in twenty-five years before as a student. Then, too, my ears and cheeks had turned bright red and given away the strong emotions I was feeling. Today I listened intently as the meeting headed on a completely different course than the one I had expected.

Both women were quite frank and had numerous comments. The woman who thought volleyball uniforms were too revealing focused at first on the book as a whole before talking about individual pieces of writing. She said that she would not allow her daughter to buy a copy of *Children of the 80's*. The book had language she didn't want to see her daughter using, but worse than that it was filled with "negative and pessimistic" writing. The principal immediately concurred with this assessment and asked a series of leading questions that surprised even me. I pretty much ignored the sweeping generalities the mother provided in response to these questions, and later she did too as she complimented specific pieces of writing. I also noticed that she had stopped just short of saying that she would fight the publication of the book. The other parent from the book club didn't find the negativism. She really enjoyed reading the book, she said, and some of the stories took her right back to her high school days. And the fifteen expletives used, scattered among the book's fifteen thousand words, didn't bother her. When she was through, I looked over at the principal to see what action he would take after hearing this evenly divided testimony. We had already been in his office for an hour. My mind wanted to line up a series of judgments that refused to line up. The principal was "a nice guy," the best of the seven I'd worked under at this school. What would he do now?

I knew he didn't like conflict. As the union's grievance chairperson, I had been in tense situations with him before, and not always in his camp. We had been professional about our differences, and none of these had seemed to be too important after the conflicts were resolved. He had asked me a couple of days before what I would do if the book were censored, and I said I would publish it independently. I guessed now that he would choose not to heighten the tension at this point but would seek compromise. I was right and I was also dead wrong. What he proceeded to do was seek a compromise, but one based on ignorance of my writing program and me.

The principal turned the discussion toward an examination of one particular piece, a humorous essay on airplane safety. Oddly, it wasn't a piece either parent had previously mentioned, and the woman who didn't want her daughter reading *Children of the 80's* had even liked this particular essay. But she agreed with the principal that one sentence was offensive: "Screw first class and to hell with your bucket of puke meals, boys." With little further discussion, he suggested that the word "screw" be deleted and substituted with "to hell" and the rest of the line reworded to accommodate the change. He asked the parents if he could suggest publishing the book provided that one change was made. I was stunned. He was only going to censor one word? What was the purpose of this? To put me in my place? To warn me for the future? The two parents showed neither strong agreement nor dissent, so he asked me the same question: Would this change be acceptable? I replied that I would have to talk with the author.

Paul Griffith, the author, was a two-hundred-forty-five-pound football tackle and a wrestler in the unlimited weight category. Currently a high school sophomore, he was easy to track down. He agreed to talk to the principal about his essay, and he came to the office surprisingly well prepared. As in the previous meeting, I contributed to the discussion as little as possible and listened intently. The meeting began with a rather humorous discussion of the sexual connotations of "screw." Paul challenged the principal to find a sexual meaning of "screw" in the dictionary on his desk. There wasn't one. The principal was nonplussed, but Paul said it didn't matter, that he knew there was at least one sexual meaning among the many meanings of "screw," and that meaning would not be very appropriate in his essay on airplane safety. He pointed out three other meanings that were more appropriate, and said he had learned in third grade that if you wanted to find out what a word meant, you read it in context.

What followed these remarks was an intense hour of debate on the First Amendment, educational philosophy, students' rights, and the power of language. I felt privileged to listen. Indeed, I was for once the only one in the room with ears and cheeks that hadn't turned red. But that didn't last long. When the principal realized that Paul would never back down on his essay, he said two things I will always remember: "Everybody realizes that it's not a question of whether to censor but of what to censor . . . this school is not a democracy for students, or for teachers either." And then he said that Paul's refusal to compromise could cause serious conflict between the principal and Mr. Kenney and affect Mr. Kenney's entire writing program. I could see from the expression on Paul's face that he understood this new line of argument and its implications. Such tactics only served to harden his resolve, and he walked proudly out of the office without giving up any ground. But as we left the meeting together, Paul told me that the word wasn't important enough to hold up the book from being published, preventing seventy other writers' work from seeing the light of day. He said, "Do what you need to do."

That afternoon I returned to the principal's office. I wanted to talk to him without parents or students present. In my hand was a book that contained no sexual innuendo or gratuitous violence, a book that promoted no racism or sexual exploitation, a book with many uplifting examples of human insight and ingenuity. Inside it there was even a student essay condemning censorship, which ended with a line from *Gone with the Wind*, a line that had been rephrased to read "Actually, to be precise, Scarlet, I really don't care." I told the principal that his decision to censor one word was silly, arbitrary, and seemed to have more to do with power than with content. I told him that he was mistaken if he thought he had a mandate from teachers to protect their programs by censoring them or shielding them from public view. Then I walked down the hall to a meeting called by the executive board of our teachers' union. The board heard me out in detail and then suggested that I publish the book immediately with the word "screw" deleted. They also decided to prepare a letter to the principal requesting a meeting to discuss his formation of an ad hoc censorship committee. The letter was signed the next day by every teacher in the district who read it.

Late that night I found myself in the school library again. I had two pages of *Children of the 80's* that needed changing. One change would have seemed unusual to the average reader— substituting "to hell" for "screw" in a humorous essay on airplane safety. The other was adding the name of Paul Griffith to the list of people the editor thanked at the beginning of the book.

Two months have passed since that night in the library. *Children of the 80's* was published amid a lot of "oohs" and "aahs" and sold quickly during the three days left of the 1989–90 school year. The principal told the president of the education association he was dismayed that so many people had felt a need to sign the request for a meeting next fall, when he had always shown a willingness to meet with anyone at any time. At a summer meeting on a different topic, he told a group of teachers that he was busy preparing a handbook of teacher conduct, so that "teachers would know what I expect of them." I immediately volunteered to form a committee that would help him draft the document.

Politics in the writing process? No, of course not. "Politics" comes from "polis," which is Greek for city, right? So politics is what those city people do. Well, be assured that politics, or the set of human relationships necessary for cities to function, is especially important to writing programs in rural areas. I write this article now so that other teachers can pick my experience apart, perhaps figuring out how the humans in this small rural school should have gotten along. Many will smile ruefully or sigh because something similar has already happened to them or to someone they know. Perhaps some will think of new survival strategies for an environment turned unexpectedly hostile to student expression. As a relatively well-known author advised some centuries ago, "Become as innocent as sheep but as cunning as wolves." I hope many writing teachers will take the steps necessary to anticipate and prevent the turmoil of censorship attempts in their districts. To be honest, I thought I had anticipated these pretty well myself. At the principal's request, and against the advice of American Library Association representatives, I had designed a parent permission slip for all the identified "objectionable" books in my classroom library of over a thousand titles. I had convinced parents and local bookstores to match the grant funding I had received to stock my classroom with those books in the first place. I had tirelessly explained my writing and literature program to the parents of each new set of students I taught. And, generally, the effort paid off. I've taught for more than a decade now at our rural school of two hundred students with only one parent complaint, and that one was easily handled.

I can foresee the occurrence of several unfortunate things next year. Our district's unique mini-grant program, which funds innovative approaches in the content areas, was the source of two of my grants and may be dismantled during the controversy to come. During contract negotiations years ago, we had pushed our school board to come up with a responsible way of handling a special block grant of state money, and the board members had responded with the mini-grant program. It has funded everything from early childhood education to atomic absorption/mass spectrometry equipment to prevention of drug abuse. What a shame it would be to lose this commitment by the district to innovation. I could list the other more obvious dangers to my writing program and to faculty-administration relations—when I've talked to teachers who have gone through similar censorship controversies, they claim that the way things once worked in their districts is irrevocably changed—but I'd prefer to look on the brighter side.

Sure, I'm a long way from teaching in a district with a serious commitment to real writing and literature programs for children in grades K–12. And sure, many of the students coming into my ninth-grade classroom have never read a book of over a hundred pages or written a real story or essay. But we have always had good parent support for our existing programs, and every day we get to teach reasonably well-behaved children still willing to learn, still full of fun and surprise. We have a very good superintendent and many very good teachers. I think I can live and let live. But I understand power and the politics of ignorance, isolation, and fear; and I won't work off in the corner where parents and other teachers don't really know what's going on, and where a principal doesn't even take the time to visit. I intend to talk up my program and my students even more than I did in past years and get more people and more relationships involved. And I might just become a bit more active in our local teacher's union . . . again.

Epilog

I did become more active in the union and was elected president in the fall. The district's mini-grant program was not dismantled, and both faculty and administration have made extra efforts to consult each other before important decisions are made. *Children of the 80's* was brought to the school board's attention, and they read it and met to discuss their findings. With the superintendent, interested teachers, and, of course, both the principal and me present, the board members had nothing but good to say about the publication. The principal himself chimed in with apparently sincere praise for its high quality.

PUBLISHING AND THE RISK OF FAILURE

MARGUERITE GRAHAM
Bread Loaf in the Schools—Bethel Project
Maine School Administrative District 44
Bethel, Maine

*I*n a recent speech, Thomas Newkirk (1990) talked of his concern about teachers who "measure themselves against standards that are not fully accurate." Newkirk was referring to the numerous books and journal articles written by or about teachers in exemplary classrooms. "If you want to advocate," he explained, "you don't tend to include the parts that are not successful." He had visited many of the classrooms that we read about, and as much as they are stimulating, student-centered, learning environments, they are also real classrooms where projects sometimes fail.

As I listened to Newkirk, I was reminded of a glowing article in the *Maine Times* about a writing project that my husband and I direct. The article described our role in introducing the writing process approach in our local school district. The year after the *Maine Times* featured the Bethel project, however, the project's major publication, *Young Voices*, failed. As Newkirk spoke, I realized that this failure was something that needed to be shared, if only as a warning to teachers who publish student writing.

In 1986, as part of the writing project, a group of teachers who met every Thursday to share student writing and discuss issues surrounding writing instruction designed a year-end publication entitled *Young Voices*. The goal of the book was to give students a purpose for revising, editing, and polishing their writing. At the end of the school year, each student whose teacher had been involved in the project would receive a copy of the anthology, which we hoped would also serve as a vehicle to help parents, administrators, and colleagues understand the role that publication plays in improving writing proficiency.

That first year the logistics of publication were quite simple. Students were given the opportunity to choose and submit one piece of writing. Each classroom's collection of student writing was gathered as a chapter and passed on to the middle-school secretary, whom we had hired to type the final manuscript. The head of the graphic arts department at the local high school agreed to allow his students to use the publication as a class project, and they would print and publish the final manuscript in book form as long as a grant paid for the cost of the paper.

During our Thursday writing support meetings, teachers in the project discussed issues surrounding publication, such as conferring with students, sense of audience, appropriate content, and final editing. At that time we did not consider the need for a central editing board for the publication since every student was included, regardless of his or her proficiency as a writer. Each teacher became the editor for his or her students' chapter in the book.

The first three hundred copies of *Young Voices* were ready for distribution the last week of school. Soon after we gave the students their personal copies, we began to receive reports full of enthusiasm and pride from teachers, students, administrators, and parents. That summer several Bethel families told us that they used *Young Voices* for bedtime reading, and a few teachers made plans to use the text for reading instruction the following fall.

By September of 1987, the number of teachers signed up to gather on Thursday afternoons had grown from fifteen to twenty. Our discussions soon moved beyond fluency, clarity, and correctness to include issues of violence and the influence of television and video on student writing. As we began to plan for a second volume of *Young Voices*, we realized that the cost of the project would grow proportionately with the number of teachers involved. We contacted the typing teacher at the high school, who agreed to have her students prepare the manuscript, thus eliminating the cost of hiring a typist. That spring, the second volume of *Young Voices* was distributed to four hundred eager children.

In the fall of 1988, the Thursday afternoon group grew in size again, and the logistics of putting together a publication that included a piece of writing from every student become more complex. The district's computer consultant suggested that technology might be the key to solving our problems. If we saved each classroom's collection of stories on a separate computer disk, he could then transfer the writing onto the school district's computer, which was hooked up to a laser printer that would produce camera-ready copy.

At this point I think we lost sight of our original goal in designing a student publication. More important, we overlooked the need to continue the discussion of publication guidelines, which we had focused on during the first year of the project. Most important, we still hadn't recognized the need to establish a central editing board. We allowed ourselves to get caught up in the momentum of management and logistics—while we continued to tell our students that good writing takes time and patience.

Some teachers still weren't comfortable using their classroom computer for publication purposes, so parent volunteers were contacted to help type stories on the word processor. As a Monday morning quarterback, I wish we had paid more attention to one parent volunteer's concern that the content of the writing she was typing was inappropriate and had far too many mechanical errors for a final draft. The teacher of this class was a first-year instructor who had only been involved with the writing project for a short time. He had not been a part of the group's earlier discussions about publication, and he had not read the writing the parent volunteer was typing. Clearly there was a lack of communication, since he had assumed that the parent volunteers would edit the student work. I believed that this was an isolated situation and that editing would not be a problem in other classrooms. Looking back, I realize that we needed to spend more time with the teachers who were new to the project, to clarify the purpose of *Young Voices* and the role of the teacher as editor and copyeditor.

Another factor we did not consider was that the project no longer needed an inclusive publication in which every student would have a piece of writing. School bulletin boards were covered with final drafts of writing, and students were submitting their finished pieces to magazines such as *Cricket* and *Voices Across the Wires*. Some classes were plastering the hallways with student print and producing their own school newspapers. Student writing was included in the weekly newsletters to parents, and students were taking their stories to read to outside audiences, such as a local senior citizens group.

Young Voices had grown into a logistical nightmare. Too many people were involved and no one was really in charge. As new teachers joined the group each year, we had overlooked the importance of reviewing and redefining guidelines for publication. And the process that was supposed to be so simple— transferring stories from the disks to the district computer's publishing program—turned out to be more complex than we had anticipated. It wasn't until the following September that the manuscript was finally ready to be printed. Then, we were in such a rush to get the project completed that as soon as the laser printer produced the camera-ready copy, we sent the pages off to be published without giving the completed text a final read.

In mid-October we received a call that the pages were ready to be collated and bound, and we planned to distribute the books by Halloween. I can still feel the excitement that filled the classroom on that Saturday morning as a team of teacher volunteers began to help with the final stages of publication. We spun through the aisles collating pages from the eighty piles and filling the counters with stacks of books ready to be punched and bound.

The following Thursday, the graphic arts teacher gave me the first bound copies of the third edition of *Young Voices* just before our afternoon writing support group meeting. I looked at the clock and knew I wouldn't have time to read the stories that my own children, Kate and Angus, had written. So, packing the books in the car, I headed for the meeting.

As soon as the others arrived we began to make plans for distributing the books to the students while Linda, a fifth-grade teacher, skimmed through one of the first bound copies. It wasn't long before the rest of us noticed Linda's generally bright expression change to one of despair. The piece she was reading not only contained multiple typing errors and spelling mistakes, it also included uncontrolled references to the violence and sex we had assumed would be avoided through conferences with students and discussions of audience.

As the rest of the group joined in the reading, several other teachers found spelling mistakes that were not typing errors, and the enthusiasm with which the group had received the publication in past years quickly disappeared. We knew that what went out to the public had to be perfect, and yet we had overlooked the important final steps of editing and proofreading.

Many of the pieces of writing were excellent contributions, but there was no one single chapter devoid of typing or mechanical mistakes. I cringed to find three typing errors in a piece written by my son's wonderful kindergarten teacher: I was the parent volunteer who had put that chapter together. More important, some chapters contained stories with content clearly inappropriate for an audience beyond the writer.

The early years of the project had been successful in encouraging all of us to allow students more time to write on self-selected topics and to share their writing with a variety of audiences. Parents as well as administrators were just beginning to understand the need for children to be allowed to write regularly, the importance of multiple drafts, and the role of invented spelling in primary children's writing.

Now, as we began to discuss the project, Caroline, a first-grade teacher, suggested that we take the book apart and distribute the K–2 chapters, since the content was clearly appropriate in all the stories, and parents and community members would be more forgiving of typing errors at the primary level. We discussed this at length and finally decided that we could not single out chapters for distribution; we could not judge one mistake as better or worse than another. As painful as the decision not to distribute the book was, we all knew we had to deal honestly with our colleagues and urge them to do the same with their students.

During the following Thursday afternoon writing support meeting, we decided to develop a set of criteria for publishing, which we then made available to other teachers in our district. Two schools were planning to put together their own anthologies, and we hoped they would be able to avoid the problems we had encountered.

I hesitate to list these guidelines because each publishing project we enter into with our students is unique and needs to have its own criteria for publication. When we made these suggestions available to other teachers in our system, we stressed the importance of letting students consider the role of and reasons for guidelines for publication. We suggested that teachers first let students come up with their own recommendations for writing that will go public: children may think of something we have overlooked, or they may develop criteria that are appropriate to their specific project.

Audience

Who will read the writing? It is essential to discuss with students who the audience is going to be for their writing. How would a piece of writing in a personal journal differ from something that was going to be read by parents, grandparents, teachers, young children, or community members? Children need to begin to anticipate how others will respond to what they have written.

Appropriate Content

What is appropriate content for a student publication with wide circulation? How do we avoid excessive violence, blood, and gore? One teacher suggested reading aloud excerpts from authors such as Dickens or Poe so that students could examine how the authors manage to frighten the reader without resorting to blood and guts. We also stressed to other teachers that if they have questions about the content of a piece of student writing that is going to be presented to the public, they should trust their instincts and get a second opinion from a colleague. This is a delicate area because no teacher wishes to act as a censor of students' writing. Perhaps the best question we can ask in such instances is "If this appeared in a professionally published book, would I want my students reading it?"

Use of Characters

When considering names for characters, we felt that it was important for students to avoid using the names of friends or acquaintances for fictional characters unless they had first shared the writing with and received permission from the real people in question. In this way, the writer avoids a situation in which he or she is seen as invading another person's right to privacy.

Conventions

The consideration of mechanics is the final stage in the process of publishing writing, and it is extremely important: readers' eyes and minds have expectations about what a printed text should look like, and errors distract attention from what the writer is saying. Our group suggested that each student should edit the writing when it is completed; then the teacher should edit the writing. To be certain that there are no mistakes, the final copy should be checked by another teacher or adult before going to a typist, and the typed copy should be returned to the student and teacher for final proofreading before it becomes part of a manuscript. This process mimics that of professional publication.

I edited this essay before submitting it to *Workshop*. Even though

I ran it through the spelling checker on my computer, Nancie Atwell caught five spelling errors when she edited the manuscript. She returned it to me for revision before submitting it to Heinemann's copyeditor. The copyeditor will go through the manuscript, make additional corrections, and return it to Nancie; she'll go through it again and return it to me so that I can make any final changes. Then, after *Workshop 3* is typeset, Nancie and a professional proofreader will each go through the page proofs to spot any errors. Little is left to chance because all of us want readers to be satisfied by what they find on these pages.

Why Publish Student Writing?

The big question teachers must ask themselves is why publish student writing at all? When our motives don't grow from students' real needs, the value of a publication venture is questionable from the start. The need to promote a writing project is not a good enough reason to create a student anthology; neither is a desire to boost teachers'—or students'—egos. Writing should go public in school for the same reasons it does outside of school: because children have something to say that they want heard. When the reasons for the writing are real, then the context for publication can also become more realistic, challenging, and satisfying.

We need to be honest with ourselves and with our students as we examine our reasons for and methods of publication. If we decide to enter into a publishing venture with our students, we must allow them the time to consider and follow appropriate guidelines for when and how they will go public as authors.

Reference

Newkirk, Thomas. 1990. Address to the Institute on Reading, Writing, and Learning, University of New Hampshire, Durham, July.

The Author Interview

BILL MARTIN, JR.

AN INTERVIEW BY RALPH FLETCHER

I recently was lucky enough to watch Bill Martin work with elementary school children and teachers during a writing institute on Long Island, New York. He is a tall and lanky man with a genuinely warm and engaging manner that might remind you of Jimmy Stewart. Bill Martin's books for children number close to two hundred and include *Knots on a Counting Rope* and *Chicka Chicka Boom Boom*. Yet while he worked with the children, he seemed less interested in talking about his own work than in hearing the stories and poems they had written. He delighted in finding beautiful language—a line here, a phrase there—in the pieces they read out loud. Later, I caught up with him at his spacious mid-Manhattan apartment.

RALPH: I'd like to talk a little bit about you as an author, and as an educator. Maybe they're not discrete things. You've been involved with whole language a long time.

BILL: Yes, but we didn't call it whole language. Back then, we called it "afternoon reading" [*laughs*], a time when we didn't have to mess with reading skills. But, of course, we *were* teaching the skills—more formidably than during the "morning reading" with its basal reader and the accompanying workbook.

RALPH: You said recently to a group of teachers: "Too often in classrooms we give kids little squirts of language. We squirt at them, and they squirt back." Could you say more about that?

BILL: Well, our language in the classroom most often is just a squirt of thought here with an answering squirt there. There isn't the satisfaction of the sweeping, strong, beautiful syntax of a story or poem, a flush of language that continues uninterrupted by carrying its own thought, creating its own anxiety, offering its own perspective.

For that reason, children should be read aloud to, many times a day. Hearing an expert read long scans of intriguing language gives children a chance, which otherwise they never have, to absorb the cadence, melody, and thought, the miracle of language. Reading instruction without read-aloud-by-the-teacher-or-other-competent-reader fails to give children the models necessary for maximum individual development. Every time we have a chance to let children choral read, or respond, or read aloud themselves, they should be encouraged to do so. Kids with a full body of poetry going at choral reading are at the heart of language learning. They'll be further engaged in choosing their favorite poems and putting them in their poetry folders. The obvious, natural result is a collection of poetry that in memory and intimate familiarity becomes a language bank for a lifetime.

RALPH: Many years ago you talked about the need to "fill the storehouse" of a child's mind with words and with stories.

BILL: Yes, assuredly.

RALPH: I saw you show one student a poem and say to him: "If you can remember this poem it'll make you a better writer." My wife, JoAnn Curtis, has a theory that the best way we can get kids to become alive to the possibilities of language in their writing is to first wake them up as *readers*. Do you think children carry over what they learn from reading into their own writing?

BILL: Yes, all of us are plagiarists. When we find a line to savor, it isn't long before it becomes part of our own work, albeit carefully camouflaged. I think it was Oscar Wilde who said that all writers are plagiarists. That is true. The intrigue of how somebody puts a sentence together lures us to try it. Sometimes I think I sound like Robert Frost, sometimes like Valerie Worth, Eve Merriam, David McCord, although I have never reached their perfection.

RALPH: So those are authors you like to emulate a little tiny bit?

BILL [*laughing*]: They are some of my models. There are many more.

RALPH: It sounds as if you're redefining plagiarism—I know you're doing it a little facetiously—almost as a kind of respect.

BILL: Yes. One of my favorite stories is of a third-grade child who wrote a poem:

> Look out little mouse in your velvet blouse
> You'll stay under cover if you are wise
> For the owl wants a dinner that's just your size
> This is a warning to you:
> Look out little mouse.

We printed it in one of our collections and gave the child credit. Then I got a letter from Aileen Fisher and she said: "Dear Bill Martin, I've been reading your *Treasure Chest of Poetry* and I was surprised when I came upon the poem (and she gave me the page number) because it sounded vaguely familiar. I went to the bookcase and pulled down a copy of a book I had done called *In the Middle of the Forest*, and there on page 72 was:

> "Watch out little mouse in your velvet blouse
> You'll stay under cover if you are wise
> For the owl wants a dinner that is just your size
> As he flutters along on feathers so soft . . .
> This is a warning to you:
> Watch out little mouse in your velvet blouse . . ."

I wrote back: "Dear Aileen Fisher, you are a marvelous teacher. Here's a child who read your poem, or heard someone read it, and loved it so much that she incubated it as her own." When she gave it back she was not plagiarizing, she actually thought she was creating an original. That is certainly one of the ways children learn language. The same is true of songs. We carry around a whole coterie of melodies and lyrics to help us make passage through the day where no passages exist.

RALPH: What do you mean by that? Just to survive?

BILL: Well, sometimes, when we're bored stiff, when we're scared stiff, when we're without recourse and stuck dead center, we begin to sing or to recite a poem and suddenly, the mind unlocks to find new ways of addressing the problem, new ways of resolving an impasse.

RALPH: In Ireland, their storytellers used to sit and tell stories again and again. It seems that in America our oral tradition is not as strong as it once was. Do you think the oral tradition can be revivified in classrooms by teachers telling stories and reading out loud to children?

BILL: Certainly we're not going to revive it as a cultural feature. The onslaught of television and programmed entertainment precludes the boredom necessary to producing a generation of storytellers. Storytelling came from periods of isolation and boredom, when people sat around the fire with nowhere to go and no entertainment aside from songs and stories they shared with each other. It was in answer to the eternal question: "How can I amuse myself? How should I live?" as William Gass asks in one of his essays. No more do we turn to storytelling as a vital, necessary mediator of life's dull rituals and mendacities. We turn to television, we turn to movies, to the theater, to the amusement park, to the ball game.

RALPH: I want to switch to Bill Martin, Jr., author. I'd like to ask about your collaboration with John Archambault. There are so many classrooms where children are trying to write together, some doing it well, though sometimes it's clearly a waste of the students' time. How do you two work so well together?

BILL: Probably we work together because of a mutual incumbency. I'm never quite sure about a manuscript—when I've finished it, when I haven't finished it. I need outside input. I need a sounding board. John provides that. When we were within a couple days of turning *Knots on a Counting Rope* in to the publisher, John called and said:

"We're not finished, Bill."

"What do you mean?" I asked.

"Well, we say the boy is blind, but we never show it. We've got to create a situation in which we can see, feel, and experience the boy's blindness."

So we finally came up with the boy asking: "I can see the horses, grandfather, but what is blue?" Thus, we addressed the question of blindness.

RALPH: It's a beautiful moment in the story. You give the reader room to make the discovery instead of hitting us over the head with it.

BILL: After we finished that rewrite John called a second time.

"We talk about the boy bonding with the horse, but there is no action to support it. There ought to be a race or something so that we see that this boy, this blind boy, has the capacity to participate competitively with sighted kids." It was then we decided to put a race in the story. It's one of the decisive climaxes in the boy's overcoming his frailty.

That's why collaboration is so important to me.

One other thing. I suppose one has to be poised for collaboration. Neither John nor I feel any competition. We've had only one or two impasses in a long arc of work, and those were resolved easily by deciding to take turns. John makes one decision, I make the next.

RALPH: How long have you known him?

BILL: I met John in 1980 at the University of California at Riverside. He was a student driver and picked me up at the airport. I was going to a conference. He knew a lot about me and I said:

"Are you in education?"

"No."

"Are you in fine arts?"

"No."

"How come you know about me?"

"Because I'm going to write picture books," John said. That interested me. He offered to show me some of his work, and when I saw his manuscripts I recognized he was a writer. Our work is better because of the collaboration.

RALPH: In *The Ghost-Eye Tree*, you use the word "foolie." It's a funny word—not really a word at all—yet everybody knows what it means. It must have been fun to invent a word to fit the story.

BILL: The word just appeared.

RALPH: Many of your books have been illustrated by Ted Rand.

BILL: I found Ted a long time ago, back in 1963 and 1964. I saw some of his work in a show and called him. He lived in Seattle. We worked by telephone for years. We never met until twenty years later.

RALPH: When I think of the three or four books of yours I particularly like—*Knots on a Counting Rope, White Dynamite and Curly Kid*, and *The Ghost Eye Tree*—those books are all about a relationship between two people where there is a kind of tension between the two. In fact, there are many similarities between *Knots* and *White Dynamite*: an older person and a younger person, the issue of fear, the dialogue back and forth between the two. I wonder why you got onto those kinds of dynamics.

BILL: A story must have something to say. I think that message is based on the characters and their inherent values. Whether or not those values are moralized is another thing. "Familyness" is key to the values in *Knots* and *White Dynamite*. Children today don't have a rooted familyness except in stories.

Yo Grocer, a forthcoming book, is about a boy's yen to work with his father instead of going to school. It's another father-son theme developed within the parameters of a Korean family, newly come to New York City.

RALPH: Did you have a strong relationship with your dad? Was he around?

BILL: No.

RALPH: So it's not something you're drawing directly out of your life?

BILL: Maybe it's a wish for a close relationship. Could be.

RALPH: Do you worry about children losing their facility with language?

BILL: No. I think that those youngsters who have a penchant for language are going to find it and fulfill it wherever they are. But I think all children can be helped by teachers who read aloud, by parents who read aloud, by people who tell stories, who act out, encourage writing. Letter writing is the perfect activity for language development. It includes both roles—that of the writer and that of the reader, intensely involved in the purposes and pleasures of language.

RALPH: What about parents? I'm thinking about a comment I heard you make to teachers: "With all the good stuff we're doing in schools, we're going to get clobbered unless we take parents along with us." Do you think parents are a crucial factor in the changes that are going on?

BILL: Yes. Parents need to get caught up in the joy of seeing their children develop the necessary skills of the culture. By having each child select a page of his best writing for each month of the school year, parents can see and appreciate the writing program. By tape-recording each month four or five minutes of a child's best reading aloud, we invite parents to see and hear the development. Acceptance of a whole language classroom depends largely on parents' understanding. That understanding is best communicated from school to home by hands-on evidence.

RALPH: You have made the point to teachers that parents need to see their children through our expert eyes.

BILL: I feel more like a teacher than a writer.

RALPH: Could you say more about that?

BILL: I enjoy creation—writing the manuscript and putting the book together—but I also get satisfaction thinking how the writing, the book, is going to be used in class.

RALPH: Do you find that being a writer creates a gap between you and the children? Or do you find it creates a closeness, a collegiality?

BILL: I found it created a real gap when I first started writing, using the name William I. Martin, Jr. No kid ever took to that. When I changed my professional name to Bill Martin, Jr., they identified. Now they all call me by the full name, Bill Martin, Jr. One time a kid said: "I know who you are—you're Bill Martin Luther King, Jr." [*Laughs.*] That came right out of his long-term memory!

References

Martin, Bill, Jr., and John Archambault. 1985. *The Ghost Eye Tree.* New York: Henry Holt and Co.

———. 1986. *White Dynamite and Curly Kid.* New York: Holt, Rinehart, and Winston.

———. 1987. *Knots on a Counting Rope.* New York: Henry Holt and Co.

ON BECOMING AN EXEMPLARY TEACHER: HAVING DINNER WITH CAROL

MARGARET LALLY QUEENAN
Stamford High School
Stamford, Connecticut

"What would you do to help teachers become exemplary?" my application form read. I didn't hesitate. "I would tell them to have dinner once a month with my cousin Carol."

Carol is usually already seated when I rush into the restaurant we have selected. I spot her easily, absorbed as always in a booklet of student writing she has brought to share. She smiles as I read, as if she has given me a gift and I am opening it. Writers' energy crackles in her students' writing. To read it is to listen to fires. I spend the dinner hour as I always do, trying to name the quality Carol has that makes the writing of her fifth graders so wonderful.

Her students are gifted, I decided the first time Carol showed me their poems, but Carol told me it wasn't so.

At dinner Carol and I talk about our students and their writing. We talk about our teaching. I listen to the silence between her comments. I want to know what she is doing in her classroom that I am not doing in mine. Her students choose their own topics. So do mine. She confers with her students. So do I. She publishes their writing. I publish my students' writing. She keeps records of her students' editing errors and holds the students responsible for the skills she teaches to them individually. So do I. She studies their writing to decide what to teach. So do I. She uses literature for writing lessons. So do I. She keeps her lessons short so students have time to write. So do I. By the time we leave the restaurant I still haven't decided what it is that makes Carol's students' writing crackle. "Next month," I promise myself. "Carol does something. . . . "

139

My son's friend, Jonathan, noticed it, too. "Is it true Ms. Brennan is your cousin?" Jonathan asked one day when he came to visit.

I nodded.

"Amy showed me her brother Tim's writing. I couldn't believe a fifth grader could write like that. But then I saw the booklet Ms. Brennan made up. It's all of a kind. So complex. How does she do that?"

How does a flame hold its shape, I say to myself.

"Well, Jonathan" (maybe explaining would help me understand), "my cousin Carol has a method—well, not a method—an attitude. She lets her students write."

Jonathan looked puzzled.

"Um. She lets them choose topics and genres."

I wasn't being brilliant.

"Her class isn't like a regular English class. My cousin Carol decides what's important and that's what she and her students spend time on."

"That's it?" Jonathan asked. "They spend time on it?"

Not exactly. How could I explain to this sincere seventeen-year-old standing in my hallway what I hadn't been able to explain to myself. Jonathan had won an NCTE Writing Award and was going to major in journalism. He wanted to know why Carol's students' writing was extraordinary. I remembered the Plato quote tacked to my classroom wall: "What is honored in a country will be cultivated there."

I sensed I was onto something: Carol honors her students' writing. It's not just the class time and the night time or the weekend time. It's the way Carol is absorbed in her students. She writes letters to them telling them what she likes about their writing. She never rests in class but constantly circulates to talk. When Carol is speaking with a student about writing, in the world at that moment there is no more important business than the student and the writing. I know this because I have felt the intensity of Carol's interest. When we are having dinner, she is just that absorbed in what I have to say.

Is that it? Had I found the answer?

As Jonathan waited, I thought back to the time we were having dinner and I had talked to Carol about my struggle to create a classroom environment that is predictable, so my students will know what to expect, and routine, so my students can concentrate on their performance instead of my choreography (Calkins 1986, 8). Carol heard in my description an absorption with my own performance and an ambivalent feeling about "predictable" and "routine." She pointed out my inconsistencies.

"My cousin Carol is honest," I told Jonathan.

Carol wouldn't tell a student that a piece of writing is fine if she didn't think so—not even to spare the student's feelings. Pretending that the writing is good when it is not announces that the student is not a writer. Carol thinks that an honest reaction has an opposite message: "You're capable. I mention your writing's flaws because I know you can fix them and I am sure you want to." Carol has two theories that she thinks all good writers attend to, so she expects that her student writers will attend to them:

1. Writers cultivate the attitude of not being satisfied. "Good enough" is not good enough.
2. Writers realize that they have much to learn from others more expert. In her classroom Carol is that expert.

Carol celebrates her students' finished work. She searches through her books for the right picture to place next to a student's story. She once made a booklet of a student's poems, wrote a dedication, and gave the poems—which she had typed—to the student as a gift. She and her friends have spent vacation days making covers for student writing. Carol organizes Authors' Nights so her students can read their writing to parents and grandparents. She prepares several such nights so only a few students need share the spotlight at a time. Her extra work reinforces the message her honesty gives: "I believe in you. You are special."

Carol is knowledgeable. She spent two summers studying with Nancie Atwell and Mary Ellen Giacobbe and never misses a Teachers College Saturday Writing Institute with Lucy Calkins. She subscribes to *The Reading Teacher, The New Advocate, Education Week, The Horn Book,* and *Language Arts,* and is a member of the National Council of Teachers of English. She reads the current works from NCTE and Heinemann-Boynton/Cook. She participates in a network with her colleagues and has a sixth-year certificate. She shares her knowledge, too, writing for publication (1988, 1989) and giving institutes and workshops for near and distant colleagues.

But what could I tell Jonathan? Carol is knowledgeable? honest? honors her students' work? shares her expertise? "My cousin Carol is a different kind of teacher," I tried again. "She only spends classroom time on what she thinks is crucially important. I've never met a teacher with such strong convictions."

I thought back to an article Carol had written, "How to Cover a Language Arts Text: Sit on It" (1988). Carol covers the language arts curriculum—literally—and teaches its skills the way she believes in—individually and privately as problems surface in her students' writing or with a mini-lesson when a problem is common to many students.

"Convictions," I told myself. "That's it." When I first started teaching in high school and the curriculum said grammar, I didn't have the courage to say, "Okay, but my way." I handed out the grammar books. Carol wouldn't have done that. I was embarrassed to tell her that I had. I knew what to tell Jonathan: "My cousin Carol expects people to have convictions."

But in saying it, I knew that there was still more to Carol's ability to be a good writing teacher. I thought again about the way Carol listens to me when we are having dinner. She wants to know how teaching is going with me. When I finally told her about giving out the grammar books, even though I don't believe in teaching grammar in an isolated way separated from writing, she wanted to know about my struggles. There was no judgment in her voice. She wondered what forces could make me feel so threatened that I would teach exercises in grammar books when I didn't believe in teaching that way.

Carol listened to my grammar book dilemma. In the air between us were the ghosts of times when I had stood alone:— Mr. Allen scolding me even though I had not stolen his pears and so had not run when my friends did; my mother protesting my silence at Lori Murphy's door, although I was not the one who had taken her school pad and so would not apologize; Sister Alice insisting that I remain while everyone else went off since I had preferred to read rather than complete the pages in my *Think and Do Workbook*. Carol and I talked about the child in me who remembers the trouble it causes to have convictions. And we talked about Maslow's hierarchy of needs. Starting in a brand new school is like beginning teaching all over again. We feel a need to earn approval. As I talked to Carol, I realized that there was a more important authority whose approval I needed: my own. And I wouldn't have it if I took sparse classroom time and squandered it. I came away from dinner with Carol that night shaking my head that I had spent the first months in my new high school position teaching in a way I didn't believe in.

Educational philosopher Maxine Greene says that students need to be engaged with in terms of *who* and not *what* they are. When I have dinner with my cousin Carol, I am engaged with.

Maxine Greene knows about that force: "It is a matter of breaking through the shells of privatism, the chill structures of autonomy, reaching out to bring something common into being." (1988, 478).

Carol engages with her students. They write so well because they write with understanding, not just of their topic but of themselves. Carol listens to writers. They begin to talk about all they didn't realize they knew about a subject, and both Carol and the writer begin to understand. I know because that is what happens to me every month when I have dinner with Carol.

"I think listening is my cousin Carol's secret," I told Jonathan.

"I wish I had a teacher like that," Jonathan said. "And I'd rather have her in fifth grade than in twelfth. By twelfth your writing is pretty much formed."

Heidi Jacobs, a theorist in the field of gifted education, spoke recently about the research on what makes a good teacher. Good teachers care. They attend to the student. They draw the student out. Heidi Jacobs was describing my cousin Carol. Teachers who hope to become exemplary should have dinner with Carol once a month—or find dinner partners like her, who know that to teach is to listen with one's whole heart.

References

Brennan, Carol J. 1988. "How to Cover a Language Arts Text: Sit on It." In *Understanding Writing: Ways of Observing, Learning, and Teaching*, 2nd ed., ed. Thomas Newkirk and Nancie Atwell. Portsmouth, NH: Heinemann.

———. 1989. "One of Us." In *Workshop 1: Writing and Literature*, ed. Nancie Atwell. Portsmouth, NH: Heinemann.

Calkins, Lucy McCormick. 1986. *The Art of Teaching Writing*. Portsmouth, NH: Heinemann.

Greene, Maxine. 1988. "Research Currents: What Are the Language Arts *For*?" *Language Arts* 65:474–80.

CALL FOR MANUSCRIPTS

Workshop is an annual about the teaching of writing and reading. Each volume is centered around a theme and features articles by teacher-researchers of grades K–8, reports of firsthand observations that show a teacher in action and include the voices and writing of students and/or colleagues. Contributors are paid. The editor is currently soliciting submissions for the fourth and fifth volumes.

Workshop 4 will address The Teacher as Researcher in the 1990s. Teachers from across the United States and Canada participated in the birth of an alternative research tradition during the last decade. Rather than viewing themselves solely as consumers of others' research, classroom teachers began to ask questions about how and why their own students were learning. And rather than attempting to establish the tight controls of quantitative modes of inquiry, teachers drew upon ethnographic philosophies and methods. They observed in their classrooms, documented their observations, and wrote about what they had discovered as members of the classroom community. The published insights of teacher-researchers have made an important contribution to our knowledge of language learning and to the development and refinement of sensible new ways of teaching language.

Workshop 4 will explore new questions and directions for teachers' research in the next decade. Such issues might include but are not limited to: the role of talk in literacy; relationships between drawing, drama, writing, reading, and talking; multi-genre writing and reading; writing and reading across the disciplines;

cross-age tutoring; the writing and reading of special needs, gifted, and ESL students; the role of the teacher's expectations, literacy, or scholarship; research collaborations between a teacher and students; and new modes of assessing writing and reading abilities. *Workshop 4* will extend the theories and models described in such texts as *Understanding Writing* (Newkirk and Atwell 1988), *Seeing for Ourselves* (Bissex and Bullock 1987), and *Reclaiming the Classroom* (Goswami and Stillman 1987). The deadline for *Workshop 4: The Teacher as Researcher in the 1990s* is August 1, 1991.

Workshop 5 will be devoted to the theme The Writing Process Revisited. Nearly a decade has passed since the publication of Donald Graves's *Writing: Teachers and Children at Work*, a book that helped change the landscape of literacy instruction in elementary schools. Practices that were initially revolutionary—allowing for invented spelling, encouraging topic choice, conducting individual conferences—are now common (though hardly the norm in U.S. schools). And even Graves himself has warned of these innovations hardening into orthodoxies or rigid prescriptions for teaching "process writing." To be truly vital these initial ideas and practices must be continually reexamined, transformed, and adapted by teachers. *Workshop 5* will examine and celebrate the evolution of writing process teaching. Manuscripts on a variety of topics are invited, not limited by the following possibilities:

- Are there new "orthodoxies" that restrict our thinking about writing instruction?
- How does talk promote and sustain student writing?
- How can children's writing profitably connect with art and music?
- How can students draw on subjects and resources in the local community?
- How can we assess student progress fairly and usefully? How, for example, can portfolios be used without creating a management burden for teachers?
- How can we respond to student writing in ways that promote growth?
- How does the media culture enhance or interfere with children's writing?
- How can we help students develop the ability to write for a range of purposes—to explain, amuse, persuade, explore, entertain, and so forth?

- As writing teachers, how can we be sensitive to cultural differences? How can we draw on these differences?

The deadline for *Workshop 5: The Writing Process Revisited* is August 1, 1992.

Manuscript Specifications for *Workshop*

When preparing a manuscript for submission to *Workshop*, please follow these guidelines:

- Contributors must be teachers of grades K–8, and submissions should be written in an active, first-person voice ("I").
- Contributions should reflect new thinking and/or practice, rather than replicate the published works of other teacher-researchers.
- Submissions must adhere to a length limit of 4,400 words per article (approximately 12½ pages typed double-spaced, including illustrations and references).
- *Everything* in the manuscript must be typed double-spaced, including block quotations and bibliographies.
- References should be cited according to the author-date system as outlined in *The Chicago Manual of Style.*
- Graphics accompanying manuscripts must be camera ready.
- Manuscript pages should be numbered consecutively.
- Send two copies of the manuscript to the editor at the following address:

> Thomas Newkirk
> Editor, *Workshop*
> Department of English
> Hamilton Smith Hall
> University of New Hampshire
> Durham, New Hampshire 03824

- Include a cover letter indicating for which volume of *Workshop* the manuscript is to be considered, as well as the author's school address, home address, home phone number, and grade level(s).
- Enclose a stamped, self-addressed manila envelope so the manuscript can be returned, either for revision or for submission elsewhere.
- If the manuscript is accepted for publication, the author will be required to secure written permission from each student whose work is excerpted.

This call for manuscripts may be photocopied for distribution to classroom teachers. The editor invites all interested teachers of grades K–8 to consider sharing discoveries about teaching and learning in the pages of *Workshop*.

ABOUT WORKSHOP 1 *AND* WORKSHOP 2

*W*_{orkshop} is an annual written by and for teachers of grades K–8, a place for teachers to share their new practices and their students' responses. The contributors are experienced teacher-researchers who avoid gimmicks and prescriptions in order to focus on how students learn the language arts and what teachers can do to help. Each *Workshop* addresses a current topic in the teaching of reading and writing. Each volume also features a discussion between an expert teacher and a professional leader, an article by a writer of children's books, and an interview with another children's author.

Workshop 1

The theme of *Workshop 1* is Writing and Literature. Its authors examine what is possible when teachers who understand real reading and writing bring them together so that students can engage in and enjoy both, draw naturally and purposefully on their knowledge of both, and discover what the authors and readers of a variety of genres actually do. A wealth of children's literature plays an essential role in their K–8 classrooms.

Readers will learn exciting new approaches to the teaching of writing and reading from teachers who understand both processes from the inside.

Contents: About *Workshop 1 Nancie Atwell* Seeking Diversity: Reading and Writing from the Middle to the Edge *Linda Rief* Casey and Vera B. *Barbara Q. Faust* An Author's Perspective: Letters from Readers *Ann M. Martin* P. S. My Real Name Is

Kirstin *Daniel Meier* The Teacher Interview: Jack Wilde *An Interview by Thomas Newkirk* When Literature and Writing Meet *Donna Skolnick* A Garden of Poets *Cora Five* Everyday Poets: Recognizing Poetry in Prose *Marna Bunce* From Personal Narrative to Fiction *Kathleen A. Moore* Historical Fiction: The Tie That Binds Reading, Writing, and Social Studies *Patricia E. Greeley* We Built a Wall *Carol S. Avery* Fossil Hunters: Relating Reading, Writing, and Science *Rena Quiroz Moore* The Author Interview: Carol and Donald Carrick *An Interview by Mary Ellen Giacobbe* One of Us *Carol J. Brennan* Process and Empowerment *Karen Weinhold*

Workshop 2

The theme of *Workshop 2* is Beyond the Basal. Although there is a definite movement toward new approaches to teaching reading, basal series are still dominant, and teachers who venture beyond them are in the minority. This book is directed to teachers who want to implement a literature-based curriculum and have questions about organizing a classroom that is not dependent on the structure created by a basal program.

The contributors to *Workshop 2* are teachers who have found practical, rewarding, and effective ways to move beyond basals and to make literature, students' responses to literature, and their own knowledge the heart of reading instruction. Readers, regardless of their experience, will be encouraged to bring literature into their students' lives.

Contents: About *Workshop 2 Nancie Atwell* Stephen and *The Haunted House*: A Love Story *Barbara Q. Faust* An Author's Perspective: The Room in Which Van Gogh Lived *Cynthia Rylant* Nebuchadnezzar Meets Dick and Jane: A Reader's Memoir *Ginny Seabrook* The Silences Between the Leaves *Marni Schwartz* Responding to the Call *Kathy Matthews* Once upon a Time in Room Seven *Kathleen A. Moore* The Author Interview: Jack Prelutsky *An Interview by Kathy Hershey* Audience: Key to Writing About Reading *Cyrene Wells* Talk: Responding to Books the Collaborative Way *Adele Fiderer* The Teacher Interview: Carol Avery *An Interview by Jane Hansen* Children as Authorities on Their Own Reading *Bobbi Fisher* Writing and Reading Literature in a Second Language *Dorothy M. Taylor* Beyond Labels: Toward a Reading Program for All Students *Joan Levy and Rena Moore* Apprenticeship: At Four or Fourteen *Linda Rief*